TIME TO SHINE AT THE RIVER SCHOOL

SABINE ADEYINKA

Chicken House

2 Palmer Street, Frome,
Somerset BA11 1DS
www.chickenhousebooks.com

First published in Great Britain in 2023
Chicken House
2 Palmer Street
Frome, Somerset BA11 1DS
United Kingdom
www.chickenhousebooks.com

Chicken House/Scholastic Ireland, 89E Lagan Road, Dublin Industrial Estate,
Glasnevin, Dublin D11 HP5F, Republic of Ireland

Cover and interior design by Helen Crawford-White
Typeset by Dorchester Typesetting Group Ltd
Printed and bound in Great Britain by CPI Group (UK) Ltd, Croydon CR0 4YY

FSC
www.fsc.org
MIX
Paper | Supporting
responsible forestry
FSC® C171272

1 3 5 7 9 10 8 6 4 2

British Library Cataloguing in Publication data available.

PB ISBN 978-1-915026-21-7
eISBN 978-1-915026-43-9

A MESSAGE FROM CHICKEN HOUSE

It's a new term at the wonderful and really rather lively River School! Join Sabine's great characters in another fantastic boarding school adventure, where friendship and fun meet a perplexing puzzle with the environment at its core. But above all this is a book about JOY and HOPE – what more can I say?!

BARRY CUNNINGHAM
Publisher
Chicken House

PRAISE FOR *JUMMY AT THE RIVER SCHOOL*

What a joyful, vibrant story! A book for the heart. Thank you Sabine Adeyinka for bringing it all back: the games, fiery chants, chasing leke leke, inter-house-sport thrills and other gems of Nigerian childhood.

EFUA TRAORÉ

I really enjoyed this delightful school story! There are midnight feasts and sporting triumphs enough to please any Malory Towers *fan – but it's also a thoughtful story of friendship, standing up for what you believe in, and why access to education matters.*

KATHERINE WOODFINE

A colourful read, it also explores the themes of justice, class and poverty.

THE GUARDIAN

Adeyinka has crafted a traditional boarding school tale, full of midnight feasts and night-time drama. However, the culturally specific class-based conflict, which sees Jummy risk her own security to help the less fortunate friend, elevates it to the top of a crowded genre.

THE IRISH TIMES

An enthralling twist on the boarding school novel . . . Adeyinka's debut is full of old-fashioned fun: midnight feasts and sporting escapades, plus crocodiles, minus mobile phones. But justice is at the heart of this book . . .

THE OBSERVER

. . . beautifully told, with powerful and emotive writing. Filled with passionate characters, this is a joyous read filled with hope.

THE SCOTSMAN

Malory Towers*-like adventure collides with themes of justice . . . an inspiring tale . . .*

BIG ISSUE NORTH

For the rivers that water our
imagination of a better world.

Also by Sabine Adeyinka

Jummy at the River School

CHAPTER ONE
TOGETHER AGAIN

I smoothed down my orange check dress, fluffed my afro and hopped towards my friend Caro. Another term at the River School – our final term in Form One. I couldn't wait! It was going to be so much fun.

We were queuing at the coach park in Lagos and I could barely keep still. The sun was blazing hot and the air was buzzing with the chatter of excited girls.

The other side of the park was full of Kingswill College boys, prancing around in khaki shorts and green polo shirts. Owolabi, my annoying neighbour, was one of them, a camera around his neck.

Caro had beautiful cornrows all neatly woven to the back and her orange check dress fitted her perfectly.

'Look!' she said, nearly yanking my arm out of its socket. 'It's Gemini and Tayo!'

Gemini's slippers made flip-flopping sounds as she ran towards us, and Tayo's arms were akimbo, her eyes dancing behind her thick spectacles.

'Hope you are ready for your final term. Delicious tests and scrumptious exams!' Tayo rubbed her hands together.

'Ahem, don't forget the first ever canoe race on the Shine-Shine River and no seniors in our rooms because Form Four girls will be prepping for mocks and Form Five girls have their finals!' Gemini's American accent was very distinct as she snapped her fingers at Tayo.

Caro giggled. I wondered how our room would be without the soft voice of Senior Funmi and the cheekiness of Ngozi. I hoped we would still get to spend time with them a little.

'It's going to be a brilliant term!' I said decidedly. 'Who wants ice lollies?'

Baba had given me money just for this, and a

crowd of girls was already surrounding the ice lolly truck that had parked in the perfect spot behind the Nile House and Zambezi House coaches. The crowd was a brilliant mix of orange and red check dresses with girls from the other houses approaching fast.

'I'll help,' Gemini offered.

'No, I can do it,' I insisted. I was almost in Form Two. I could handle a bunch of rowdy girls hustling for ice lollies.

I somehow managed to get to the front of the crowd and shout out my request, but when it was time to collect my four jumbo orange ice lollies, four girls pushed ahead of me. Three of them were in red Zambezi dresses and one was in Nile House like me. I knew her a little – her name was Ola and she was in Form Three.

'Hey!' I started to protest but they all turned towards me hands on hips, daring me to continue. All four of them had their hair gelled to the max and pulled back, making their faces as taut as a longbow set to fire an arrow.

I gulped and was just about to step away when someone's arm went over my head and collected my four lollies.

I turned to find an unfamiliar and very tall girl in an orange check dress. She was taller than any senior I had ever seen, but all the seniors had already been in school for a week studying for their final year exams. Who was she? Her face was unsmiling and she had deep-set eyes that seemed to suck you in but told you nothing.

When she handed me the lollies, the four girls looked at her up, then down.

'Ola, do something about this little Nile mouse and her giraffe friend,' said one of the Zambezi girls.

Ola hesitated.

'Unless you don't want to be part of the Atlantic Four?' the girl went on. 'Maybe we were much better as a group of three. Am I right, girls?'

'Look here, we are the Atlantic Four!' Ola said, finally finding her voice. 'When you see us coming, you move out of our way next time. Understood?' She was trying to sound menacing but I was not convinced.

The tall girl who had helped me didn't even wait for Ola to finish – she just walked away.

'Thank you!' I said after her but she was already too far ahead. A whistle blew and that meant it was time to get on the coaches.

'It's crazy out there,' I said as I rejoined my friends and handed out ice lollies. 'If it wasn't for a new girl, we wouldn't have got any.'

The whistle blew again. We tore open our ice lollies and rushed towards the coach.

Mrs Aliu, our Nile housemistress, stood at the front counting us before we were allowed on.

'Finish those ice lollies outside,' she said. Her high-pitched voice showing some irritation.

We joined a group of girls doing the same.

'We're going to get rubbish seats now.' Tayo was annoyed.

'It was worth it,' Caro said, licking her lolly and tapping her foot to some imaginary music.

'Ola Martins, will you get back here this minute!' Mrs Aliu called.

Ola's Zambezi friends had tried to sneak her on to their own coach. Their housemistress, Mrs Kolawole, who was laughing and chatting, was oblivious to the scam about to take place under her nose. Mrs Aliu was much more astute and had spotted the splash of orange like an eagle sifting out its prey.

'Ah look at this girl o. You want to disgrace me?' Mrs Kolawole said in her deep smoky voice. 'Return to your house this minute. I trust Mrs Aliu will deal with you.' Mrs Kolawole was our Yoruba teacher and she was known for her sense of humour. She was trying very hard to be taken seriously by Mrs Aliu, but discipline was not her strongest point.

Ola's three friends got on their coach without looking back at her even once.

We'd just finished our lollies when a car screeched to a halt beside us and a girl tumbled out. It was our friend Lola. All of us rushed towards her.

'There was so much traffic,' she gasped, yanking her suitcase out of the boot. 'I can't believe how late we are. We left on time but who could have predicted a herd of cows deciding to sit on the road!'

Tayo was right – there were hardly any good seats left on the coach. We all had to sit with random people. Caro was in front of me – beside the mysterious tall girl. I smiled at her but she quickly turned to face the window.

Lola, Gemini and Tayo managed some seat swaps and soon we were all near each other. There was only one spot left behind Caro but it was next to Ola Martins. She was still staring after the Zambezi coach as it pulled out of the station. I had already had enough of her and we hadn't even arrived at school yet. I sat down reluctantly.

'I hope we are still in the same room,' Caro said, turning round to me.

'Me too!' I looked anxiously at Mrs Aliu who I could see was just about to do the roll call.

'Keep an open mind,' Tayo warned, pushing her glasses up her nose. 'You know the rooms will be different because the seniors are in their own rooms to study.'

'I shall start with Nile House room one,' called Mrs Aliu from the front of the coach. 'When you hear your name, say "Present Ma".'

Before she could continue, to our surprise, there was a knock on the door of the coach and a group of Kingswill boys bundled on. I groaned when I saw one of them was Owolabi. They spoke to Mrs Aliu, every single one of them dwarfing the Nile housemistress in her purple kaftan. I couldn't hear what they were saying.

'Well girls,' she said, turning to us, 'these are members of the press club at Kingswill College and they would like to take a picture of you all. It's for an article for their school newsletter about how our two schools are reducing the amount of traffic on the roads by using coaches.'

Owolabi grinned at me.

I groaned again and thought everyone would join in, but almost all the girls began to rearrange their dresses and put on the most elaborate smiles. I rolled my eyes at Tayo who I was sure would be just as irritated as I was, but even she removed her thick glasses and flashed all her thirty-two teeth at Owolabi.

I looked at Ola Martins beside me. She hurriedly spit on her palms and used it as a gel for her hair. Then, she pushed herself towards me to make sure she got into the shot.

I shrugged and grimaced into Owolabi's camera.

When the boys left, Mrs Aliu launched back into her roll call, and called out Caro's name right after mine and Gemini's.

'Yes!' Caro and I cried out. We were together! I was over the moon.

Mrs Aliu shot us a look.

'I mean, Present Ma!' Caro corrected herself.

Mrs Aliu went on. 'The two seniors in Nile House room one have been replaced by Tayo Coker—'

Gemini squealed with delight and nearly fell out of her chair.

'Present Ma.' Tayo smiled wide as she and Gemini high-fived.

'. . . and Dongo Karkananshi in Form One O.'

'Present Ma,' the tall girl beside Caro answered in a low rasping voice and turned to face the window again.

So she was in my room and in my class. I wasn't sure about it. Sure, she had helped me with the ice lollies but she seemed quite strange and unfriendly. I didn't want her to spoil the flow of Nile House room one, the best room in all of River School.

Finally, the roll call was done. Mrs Aliu tapped the driver's shoulder. 'Oya Baba Wale, let's go.'

The coach purred to life and we all drummed on the windows. I knew the exact song we were going to sing and I joined in with all my might.

Baba Wale, show us your driving power!
God be with us this hour!

Dongo looked at us blankly. I thought back to my first time at the River School and felt for her. Perhaps she was just homesick.

'Don't worry,' I reassured her. 'You'll soon know all of the songs.'

CHAPTER TWO
UP THE RIVER

It seemed that no matter how hard I tried, I could never stay awake for the full forty-five-minute ride to the River School. The smell of freshly baked bread woke me up as we passed the Redbrick Bakery. Light-grey smoke from its chimneys swayed into the clouds.

The coach mounted the bridge and even Tayo stopped talking as Shine-Shine River came into view. We all jostled to be the first one to see our beloved river. Many girls pulled down their windows and put their heads out.

The smell that hit us before we could even see the river was nothing short of disgusting. It was as if a million rotten eggs had been unleashed. The smell went straight to my stomach and was soon rising up into my throat.

Everyone began to close the windows and cover their noses with their white under-tops.

I leant forward to see the river for myself.

As usual, the sun was shining over it, but this time the river didn't shine back. There were no Leke Leke, the white egrets that usually graced the banks of the river with their long necks and skinny legs. The array of fishermen's canoes along the waterside were nowhere to be seen. What had happened here?

'It smells like death!' Gemini gasped, breaking the silence.

Everyone started talking through covered mouths.

'Girls, I wouldn't worry too much about the smell. It will disappear as quickly as it appeared, I am sure.' Mrs Aliu tried to sound convincing but she looked very worried herself.

'It smells a thousand times worse than the Lagos canal!' Tayo cried indignantly, leaping out of her seat.

'Madam Tayo, please sit down!' Mrs Aliu warned.

'But Ma, look over there!' Tayo pointed to a large white-chested bird perching on the branch of a leafless tree.

'What about it?' Gemini said.

Tayo rolled her eyes. 'If I am not mistaken, it's an African fish eagle and I have never seen one here before. It eats fish of course but . . .'

Tayo paused and looked around at us all.

'It . . . also . . . eats . . . Leke Leke!'

We gasped in horror.

There was no keeping us quiet now. Our precious white egret, which we sang for each time we crossed the bridge, was nowhere to be found and in its place was this big fat eagle.

At last, we reached the welcoming gates to the River School and everyone cheered as they opened before us. At least our school did not disappoint. We waved at Baba Green, the school caretaker, and he waved back, his lanky frame disappearing into the distance behind us as the coach drove up the long driveway. We were extra grateful for the lemon and orange trees that lined the road. The beautiful scent filled the bus.

The coach parked in its usual spot in the manicured square outside our principal's white cottage. Several other coaches had already arrived but we were not the last. The red hibiscus and yellow allamanda that surrounded the cottage seemed brighter than ever and Mrs Ayodele – Princey, as we called her – came out of her cottage to greet us. She was dressed in a bright orange kaftan and Barky, her black-and-white cat, stalked about beside her, tail upright and assured.

We tumbled off the coach. It was as though every flower on earth was in bloom at the River School. Gone were the hustling and bustling sounds of Lagos car horns and people selling their wares and in came the crickets, chirping of birds and the flip-flopping of a thousand slippers.

'Hey Jumoke, stop daydreaming and take care of your new room-mate.' Mrs Aliu's voice pierced my thoughts.

'Yes Ma!' I said proudly. 'Dongo, get your things and follow me.'

It felt really good to be the one showing a new girl around.

'Don't worry if you struggle with the luggage,' I said, remembering how I had struggled the first time I'd arrived at the River School. 'We can stop and rest.'

Dongo shrugged and put her bucket, which had lots of tools inside, on her head like the street hawkers in Lagos. Then she carried her suitcase in one hand and her travelling bag in the other. She didn't even need to hold on to the bucket. It was as steady as the stacks of bread on a bread seller's head. If I thought she looked tall before, she now looked like a giraffe taking a leisurely walk in her tropical garden.

Caro and I stared at each other. Dongo was going to take getting used to, I thought.

We made our way to our dorms, passing the dining hall with its metal roof drooping over the concrete walls like an unwilling coat.

'This is where all the action happens,' Caro said. 'The noise when everybody is inside is louder than on a Saturday market day.'

'Plus, the food isn't half bad, except for the

weevils in the beans that they serve every resumption day. It's like they want to remind us we are no longer at home,' I added.

'Do they serve tuwo shinkafa?' Dongo asked in her low voice.

'What is tuwo shin . . . whatever you called it?' I asked.

'Never mind—'

'They don't serve it,' Caro put in, 'but I know it is mashed sticky rice and you eat it with okro soup.'

Dongo looked at Caro in disbelief. 'How do you know?'

'My mother is not from the north but she can make it very well,' Caro explained.

'Well, we better hurry, we are the last to get to the dorms,' I said, noticing everyone passing us by. We quickened our steps, Dongo having no trouble. The bucket on her head did not shift even a tiny bit!

When we got to the dorms, we stopped suddenly – staring in wonder, our mouths dropping open. Dongo put down her bucket.

The dorms had been transformed. Every

cottage had received a fresh lick of paint in the colour it represented and the names of the six houses – Nile, Niger, Congo, Zambezi, Limpopo, Senegal – were bolder than before. But that wasn't what made us stop in our tracks. The wild scrub-land bush in the centre of the dorms, which we had to tame every Thursday during manual labour, was now a beautiful garden.

'Wow!' Caro and I said together.

Each house had flowers in its section to match the colour of the house. My eyes went from house to house.

Niger House, which was next to Nile House, had vibrant green palms, with huge leaves. Next was Senegal with a bed of blue diamond flowers while Congo had yellow allamandas glowing in the afternoon sun. Limpopo's purple orchids were planted in pots and a young red hibiscus bush was starting to bloom outside Zambezi. A large yellow butterfly flew past us and landed on one of the orange heliconia blossoming beautifully in front of Nile House. I beamed with total satisfaction.

'As soon as I'm unpacked, I'm coming back

outside to walk through the gardens,' Caro said in a determined voice.

'But before that, I'll race you for the best bed,' I shouted over my shoulder as I rushed up the Nile House stairs.

CHAPTER THREE
ROOM FOR EVERYONE

'Hello strangers!' Tope, our Form Three room-mate, greeted us with a smile.

She was wearing a badge that said 'Room Captain'.

She caught me looking at it and grinned. 'I have powers now!' she chirped. 'And look how clean our room is. My dad has been beautifying the school and I've been doing my bit here.'

Our room really was clean for a first day. Tope's dad was the caretaker Mr Lawanson, who we called Baba Green, though never in front of her. The window louvres and the lockers shone. I could see Tope had been hard at work.

'So you are Dongo Karkananshi? Welcome to the best room in the whole school.' Tope shot her hand out and, after a moment's hesitation, Dongo shook it.

Gemini, who was swinging her feet back and forth on her bed, whistled. 'You're in Form One?!' she asked incredulously. 'But you're so tall!'

Caro shot Gemini a look. 'Yes, she is in Form One. Let's get you settled, Dongo. You can take the bed below me.'

I went over to the bed below Gemini's – the one I'd had for two terms now – to unpack but before I could, Tayo barged into the room with Lola and Michelle. They were giggling so hard.

'I am not responsible for the fake addition to your precious room list o!' Lola managed to get her words out as tears of laughter ran down her face.

Tope ran out to check and came back looking quite amused too. 'They have added their names to our room!'

Michelle and Tayo were best friends. We called them the twins even though they looked nothing like each other. They were always together except on the coach to school because Michelle lived at the River School with her mother, the French teacher. She came over and gave me a big hug and two kisses, one on each cheek.

'Ah *mon amie*, Jummy! So good to see you.' Her eyes danced around behind her red-rimmed spectacles and her two plaits sat neatly on her shoulders. 'I have missed everybody!'

'I bet you played with Barky so much you didn't miss us one bit!' Gemini added and we all laughed.

Michelle loved Princey's cat so much that we always said if she went missing we would know who had taken her.

'I cannot wait for assembly tomorrow,' Lola said excitedly. 'Princey will announce all the fun things to look forward to this term like the canoe race between the north and south sides.'

Dongo's eyes lit up for the first time since I had met her. 'I know about canoes. My father is . . . was . . .' Her face fell. She zipped up her empty suitcase, then lay down on her freshly made bed reading an old notebook. She was done unpacking and I hadn't even started.

'Last year we had a picnic in the playground overlooking Shine-Shine River. That was a blast!' Gemini jumped on her bed with such gusto that the whole bunk shook.

'More like smell-smell river!' Tayo said.

'The seniors are here!' Lola interrupted, pointing at the window.

Sure enough, coming towards Nile House were a bunch of seniors in their orange check skirts and blouses. Studying for mocks and finals was serious business. They had everything they would need to both study and sleep hard. Some of them had tied wrappers around their housewear, some carried pillows and big textbooks in addition to their school bags.

We ran outside and cheered their arrival. They looked so tired from all their studying, but our arrival seemed to rejuvenate them.

Senior Moradeke swayed her hips from side to side as she belted out a popular Nile House chant. We all joined in.

Winner ooo Winner!
Winner ooo Winner!

Nile House, you don win o, Winner!
Pátápátá you go win for ever, Winner!

We hugged them and helped them carry their things.

'My *ẹ̀fíkòó* runner!' Ngozi had called me that since I won the race for Nile House two terms ago.

'How is our old room?' Senior Funmi smiled. Her hair was in its usual neat cornrows pointing to the sky and a beautiful gold heart pendant hung on a very delicate necklace around her neck.

'We are doing great. I want to talk to you both about something please . . .' Tope said as she, Senior Funmi and Senior Moradeke walked away.

'Tope has already started bossing us around,' Gemini was saying to Ngozi.

Other girls came out to greet their former room-mates and there was a lot of noise in the house. I had really missed this place. Even Dongo who had only been here a few hours didn't look too out of place. That was Nile House for you, a second home for us all.

CHAPTER FOUR
UNDER THE STARS

'I hope you don't think the room one club are getting the box room this time around?' Ola Martins said from inside the box room.

Bukky and I had come to get it ready for our usual start-of-term midnight feast – and we always had it in the box room that held all our empty suitcases at the end of the dorm. Bukky, with her larger-than-life smile and jumbled-up teeth, was the first friend I had made at the River School and it was at my first midnight feast. It was one of the highlights of the term, all of us huddled together sharing good home-cooked food in the middle of the night.

'Room one club?' I stared at her blankly.

Ola was plaiting the hair of one of her Zambezi friends who was seated on a metal bucket with a pillow on top. The other two Zambezi girls were there too, sitting down on people's suitcases and crushing them in the process.

We didn't know how to answer her because she was a Form Three girl and it had also never occurred to me that others may want to use the box room.

'Don't you know that's what we call you and all your attachments?' the girl getting her hair done said meanly. The middle part of her hair was yet to be plaited and so it stood up in the air making her look like a cockerel.

'Look, there's only one club worth talking about at the River School and that's us. The Atlantic Four. My name is Yinka and I'm the leader of it.' She stood and came towards us. 'You know how the Atlantic Ocean is bigger than the Shine-Shine River? Well, that's how much bigger we are than anything around here. Now, Ola, finish my hair so you can start on the others.'

'She's the one who is an attachment!' Bukky

said crossly, as we went to get Gemini and the other Form Two girls to reason with her.

When we arrived with the Form Two girls, the door of the box room was locked and so we knocked.

'Yinka said that erm . . . what should I say again?' the speaker attempted timidly behind the locked door.

'Say Miss Yinka this time,' we heard her prompt.

'Miss Yinka is preparing for her midnight feast in the box room.'

We all burst into fits of laughter.

'What is so funny?' Yinka barked, barging out of the door, her hair still only half done.

'Look girl, we don't need to fight about it. Can't we share the box room? How many people have you got?' Gemini was being uncharacteristically cool.

'I don't want to share anything with your stinking room one club! I have my own sophisticated club here,' Yinka snapped.

'Yes, we are the Atlantic Four and we plan on doing our hair and talking all night in the box room,' Ola added.

All of us looked at each other and tried to not laugh again.

'Wait, what? You're not allowed to use our box room! Go and use Zambezi's box room.' Lola was not finding it funny.

'But I'm in Nile House so I have the right to use the box room! And we got here first!' Ola snapped back. Her three friends stood there nodding, their arms crossed.

'What have we got here, a fight on the first day of term?' Someone must have alerted Tope because she came just in time before the cool switch turned off in Gemini's eyes.

'Ah, if it isn't another room one club member!' Ola said.

'Please say something else,' Lola yawned.

'I am sure we can come to some agreement,' Tope was just saying when the bell went for lights out. You could hear the groans across all the dorms.

Tope dispersed the crowd that had formed and we headed back to our rooms. Would we have a midnight feast tonight or would we have to eat our home-cooked food in our rooms? It would be very unsatisfying indeed on our first night. Worse – there might be no midnight feast at all!

I sighed grumpily as I got into bed.

'You know what they say Jummy, every disappointment is a blessing,' Tope said as she switched off our room light.

Over the noise of the crickets, I listened out for the owl that I sometimes heard outside my window but there was nothing. I hoped he hadn't found another tree to live in. It had been a long day and I drifted easily into a deep sleep . . .

It didn't seem long before someone was tugging at my arm.

'Jummy, wake up.' It was Caro. She was giggling softly. 'Tope wants us all out on the lawn.'

I sat up to look out of the window. It was pitch black. A single light shone in the distance from Princey's cottage.

'What? It can't be morning yet,' I protested.

The room door creaked open.

'Come on outside,' Tope urged us in a gentle whisper.

Dongo and I got out of bed at the same time. Gemini stirred in her bed and Tayo stood up stretching and yawning loudly.

'Well, this better be good.' Gemini was obviously irritated at being woken up.

Tayo led the way and Caro, Dongo, Gemini and I followed her to the Nile House lawn.

My mouth fell open. I looked to the others. Caro's mouth had dropped too, there was a twinkle in Gemini's eye and even Dongo had a hint of a smile. We were as quiet as if an angel had struck us mute.

The lawn was lit by several torches and candles stuck on the front and back porch ledges. There were two blankets spread across it and food laid out, with little paper plates and cups. It wasn't a lot of food but under the night sky lit with a thousand stars, it was magical.

'Welcome to the Nile House midnight feast,' Tope said.

We clung to her every word. I thought it was only Senior Moradeke that could command our attention that way.

'I got us some Redbrick Bakery treats but if you

have any food you'd like to share please bring it and let's have a great time together.'

Our whispers and chuckles filled the midnight sky and the stars lay scattered above us like they too were having their own picnic.

On our blanket lay chinchin, plantain chips and a few bottles of fizzy drinks. I added the fried chicken my mum had made, Caro put in a packet of biscuits and Dongo a snack made from groundnuts which she said was kuli kuli. They looked like brown wooden sticks.

Gemini wobbled towards us, holding her dress up like a bucket, and emptied the contents on to the blanket dramatically. All sorts of American treats lay before us – cookies, candy and chips to feed an army. We began to rip everything open.

'Oh the Redbrick packaging has changed,' I whispered. 'It's so tough to open.' It finally gave way, making a popping sound.

Tayo examined the bag suspiciously. 'They've used a thicker plastic material to ensure the chinchin stays fresh.' She bit into some. 'It has worked. Hmm!' She eyed the bag again.

Everyone now wanted to try the new chinchin.

Gemini grabbed my bag when the packets had run out and I made a face at her.

'It's the same with the plantain chips,' Caro observed. She put a chunk into her mouth and made such a crunchy sound that we all reached out for some.

'I wonder what they did with all the old packets,' Tayo said, reaching forward to pick up Dongo's snacks. 'But anyway, this is better – I love kuli kuli.'

Dongo's face lit up. 'You know it?'

'She knows everything,' Michelle said as she joined us at our little corner of the lawn.

'My neighbour in Lagos is from the north,' Tayo explained, 'and she sells kuli kuli from her house. It's made from groundnuts isn't it?'

Everyone took a stick and we all crunched away loudly. It was like peanut butter turned into a biscuit stick and I loved it. So I took another one.

There was nothing we didn't talk about. Everything from the latest dance moves to all the new TV adverts we saw over the hols. Tayo tried to bring up the smelly river again but nobody wanted to talk about that.

‘My older sister came to the River School and she would have told me if the river ever smelt, and I have never smelt anything that bad in all my life,’ Tayo tried.

‘Was it really that bad?’ Bukky asked. ‘I wish we got to pass over the river like you do from Lagos. All we get to see is wild bush from Ibadan.’

‘You should thank your lucky stars. I’m telling you, it was bad. There were no Leke Leke and the river smelt like rotten eggs.’ Tayo pinched her nose with one hand and held her kuli kuli in her other hand. Michelle grabbed it from her and put it straight into her own mouth.

We laughed till our sides began to hurt.

One minute there were stars shining, the next there were dark clouds and a torrent of rain pouring down so fiercely, there was barely enough time to gather all the picnic things. Dongo picked up the blanket, shook it and turned it into an umbrella. We all huddled under her tall arms and ran to the covered corridors.

The crashing of the rain and the smell of it as it hit the grass made us all just stand there and watch it fall. We were still huddled together under the blanket even though we no longer needed it. We knew the magical night had come to an end. But it would never be over in our hearts. We'd remember this for a lifetime.

CHAPTER FIVE
WHAT'S UP FOR THE TERM

The next morning, I stood on the front porch of Nile House watching others go by for breakfast. The rain had poured all night and the orange heliconia looked thoroughly satisfied, the soil lush with moisture. A light wind blew, and bugs and creepy-crawlies littered the pathway that led to the dining hall. I was the first one ready this morning. Caro had given me water from her large bucket because the taps had been running slow. She had queued for a full thirty minutes to get water.

'Don't waste your time, have some of mine,' she had said. 'The water is crawling out like an old tortoise.'

I was just about to gently tap one of the millipedes so that it would wriggle its many tiny legs and curl up into a ball when someone called out behind me.

'Chief Grubido!'

I suppose I deserved that. I must look quite desperate for breakfast standing out on the porch all by myself. I turned to find Bukky and Flanky smiling as they walked towards me. Flanky hadn't been on the coach because she lived at Kingswill College where her dad was principal. She was lean and tall with a jet-black bob.

They both looked quite smart in their green-and-white cotton uniforms, which were perfect for the humidity at this time of the year. Bukky wore brown jelly sandals for the rainy weather.

'Nice shoes,' I remarked.

'You know me, always the pragmatist,' Bukky retorted.

'It is too early for big, big English!' Caro came up behind us with Dongo.

We laughed as we began the short walk to the dining hall.

Dongo was not yet in school uniform. She

would have to wait for the class teacher to give it to her. She wore a white cotton dress that fitted her so nicely. It stopped just shy of her knees and her legs went on for miles. She had the richest cornrows all woven to the back.

'Dongo, you look lovely,' Bukky said kindly.

'Thank you,' Dongo said, hunching over and looking down at the ground as if she had kept something there.

'Tell me, what form are you?' Flanky asked.

'Form One O,' Dongo replied, looking as if she was already anticipating the shock.

'Thank you! Thank you! Thank you!' Flanky cried, throwing her arms around her. 'It's been really lonely up here. We shall be best pals at the back of the Form One O line.'

Dongo smiled awkwardly and straightened her hunch just a little.

As we approached the dining hall, the noise of over 500 girls without seniors to control them was immense.

'I will miss eating with all the seniors this term, they keep us sane,' I said.

'Well, I shall not miss them. They normally

finish all the tea with their giant mugs,' Bukky grinned.

Caro gave Dongo a reassuring look.

We made our way to Mama Tea, the tea lady, who served us piping-hot sweet milky tea. We were just about to return to our seats when there was a lull in the noise.

The cause of the silence was Princey in a bright green kaftan, with all the housemistresses. The other five women towered over Nile House's Mrs Aliu, but she walked proudly wearing a flowing orange kaftan that left you in no doubt of the house she represented.

'Good morning, girls.' Princey's smooth voice boomed across the dining hall.

'Good morning, Mrs Ayodele,' we chimed together.

'You may all be seated.' She turned and nodded at us, and I was relieved. For a moment, I thought we'd have to stand there with our cups of tea for ever.

We made our way to the Nile House area and dispersed to our different room tables.

'Welcome back to third term, which is always

special at the River School,' Princey went on. 'We can't ignore the strange smell coming from the river and we have been waiting for a visit from the River and Water Authorities. The good news is with the water shortage, they have promised to visit this morning which is why, instead of our usual welcoming assembly, we decided to bring assembly to you in the dining hall.'

A murmur broke out around the hall and Princey gave us her firm stare, which made us all quiet again.

'Congo, Zambezi and Senegal had no water this morning and the rest of you had a slow flow which is obviously not ideal. In the meantime, I would like to draw your attention to the extensive work carried out on your house gardens during the holidays by Mr Lawanson.'

We belted out loud cheers and clapped to show our appreciation.

I looked at Tope now. She was beaming with pride.

'In addition to this, we have also cleared the portion of land behind Nile and Niger House for everyone to plant corn. Each housemistress will guide you in your planting, but the rest is up to you. We will be looking at the best corn yield at harvest time. There will be a trophy for the best produce and roast corn will be served after harvest.'

We cheered again and this time, Princey let us chat for a while.

'I l*ove* roasted corn!' Caro said a little too loudly just as the noise was going down. Everyone heard her and we all broke out into chuckles.

'And of course, we have the first ever canoe race between the north and south sides of the river. Both Kingswill College and our school fall under the south side and so we will come together to support our rowers, whoever that may be.'

I looked at all my room-mates' faces. They were as excited as I was. Tayo's eyes were like hair beads dancing around behind her glasses. I knew she would have lots of questions.

'It is great for our two schools to collaborate and strengthen relationships. At the moment, it looks like Mr Lawanson and one other adult will represent the south side.'

This caused the loudest cheer yet. We were just settling down when there was the sound of a large vehicle arriving outside the dining hall.

Someone banged a door shut and we heard footsteps marching towards us.

A large woman in khaki trousers and jacket strode through the dining hall. She held a pair of thick gloves in her hands and looked formidable with her short afro and black boots. As she walked past our table, I saw medals on the front of her jacket and the words ‘Fire Chief’ on the back. I imagined her in charge of a fire truck, driving through the town, putting out fires and saving lives. Her arms looked strong enough to row ten canoes all at once.

‘I would like to introduce you to Fire Chief Moni Ogunbanjo,’ Princey announced. ‘She has kindly agreed to provide us with water this afternoon and for the rest of the week if this water shortage continues.’

Chief Ogunbanjo smiled at us. ‘Good morning, girls! It is a pleasure to be of service to you. I will arrive after lunch and I understand I’ll be starting with Nile House.’ She looked at Princey who nodded her approval.

‘Once you see our red truck parked outside,

please bring your buckets and we will be happy to fill them up. Do you have any questions for me?'

There was a deafening silence as we all looked around the hall to see if anyone dared ask any questions. A hand went up. It was Tayo. Only Tayo would be so bold as to ask a question at first assembly. The way she peered above her glasses made her look very serious indeed.

'When we crossed the bridge over Shine-Shine River in the coach, it smelt so bad. Do you think that's why we have almost no water coming through the taps?' Her voice was confident and she looked straight at the fire chief.

'What an intelligent observation!' the chief said, looking quite impressed. 'Yes, there have been complaints from the fishermen and others who use the river regularly that the smell is unbearable and it is affecting the fish and other aquatic animals.'

Tayo looked around the room as if to say 'I told you so' to the doubters.

Chief Ogunbanjo smiled. 'Like the fire department, your school gets its water supply from the river. We may have to stop that for a while and get water from the borehole situated between your school and the Redbrick Bakery. We hope to get to the bottom of it soon. In the meantime, please try to use water sensibly and only when necessary.'

Tayo put her hand up again. The fire chief smiled.

'Ahem! Ma, what if the river is so polluted that the canoe race can't take place?' Tayo blurted out.

This caused an even louder buzz.

'That is enough! Please settle down, girls!' Princey's voice was now very stern.

We calmed down, but I was not settled at all. I mean, whoever heard of a canoe race without water?

CHAPTER SIX
PEARLS AND NECKLACES

We spent the first school day cleaning our classrooms and getting them ready for the term. Mrs Folawiyo, our class teacher, put Bukky in charge and she took her responsibilities very seriously.

Dongo and Flanky were chosen to renovate the blackboard with black paint on account of their height. By the time they finished, Dongo's white dress was spotty black and Flanky had black dots on her white face. They looked like a pair of clowns about to put on a show.

I dusted the window louvres with a few other girls who were smart enough to wear aprons they got from the cleaning cupboard in the home economics, lab but the rest of us were rather dusty indeed.

Every activity was an opportunity to drum on our desks and sing popular songs.

We finished at break time when Rashidat, who had gone to get our midday snack, returned to the classroom with a steaming bowl of glistening puffpuff. The smell had wafted into the air even before her arrival and everyone rushed towards her.

'Hold on everyone, let's be civilized. Form a queue behind me.' Bukky was still in boss mode.

'You are no longer our oga, cleaning has finished.' This protest came from Chichi, who was the oldest girl in our class and never let us forget it.

'You people are not serious. It seems like you want cold puffpuff,' Rashidat said, shaking her head at us fondly. That was all we needed to hear.

We were enjoying the crispy puffpuff when Mrs Kolawole, the Yoruba teacher and Zambezi housemistress, poked her head into the class.

'*Ẹ fún mi ní ìṣẹ́jú márùn-ún.*' Her voice sounded

as if she had just eaten a dry piece of yam.

A few of us looked to Bukky to interpret.

'She wants us to give her five minutes,' Bukky said.

'Ah we can give her one whole hour sef,' Chichi said, making all of us chuckle. Chichi was an Igbo girl, from the east of Nigeria, and didn't like Yoruba lessons at all. Last term, she'd screamed when the Yoruba teacher gave out our end-of-term test papers. She then drew a face in the zero she'd scored and stuck the paper on the blackboard. Mrs Kolawole had laughed so much she had to sit down.

After a few minutes Mrs Kolawole entered the classroom with a large box. She wore a blue flowing bubu with silver headgear tied elaborately.

'This term,' she announced, 'we are going to focus on the speaking aspects of Yoruba language which is what we speak in this part of Nigeria.'

Chichi and a few others groaned.

'*Ẹ panu dé!*' Mrs Kolawole demanded and the class was quiet again.

She set the box on Bukky's table and produced an item of clothing from it.

'*Kí le léyìí?*' Mrs Kolawole said, looking for someone to tell her what she was holding.

Bukky shot up her hand. '*Aṣọ òkè ni*, which is a handwoven cloth.'

'*Ẹ pàtẹ́wọ́ fún ọmọ náà.*' Mrs Kolawole told us to clap for Bukky.

Next, she produced a small cap and all our hands went up. She was very happy that Chichi's hand went up too.

'*Fìlà.*' Chichi said it as if she were speaking English.

'*Ah ah Ẹ wo ọmọ yìí!* This is not a European language where you open your mouth small. Come on! Open your mouth wide. Oya everybody say, "*Fìlà!*"'

We opened our mouths as wide as we could and shouted, '*Fìlà!*'

'*Eh-hen! Àwọn ọmọ rere bí iyán!*' She declared we were as good as pounded yam, which was the best compliment in all of Yoruba land.

Mrs Aliu pushed her head through the door just as Mrs Kolawole held out a shiny string of black pearls.

She asked us to work in groups of four, taking

an item of interest out of the box and discussing it in Yoruba.

'No English!' she insisted before joining Mrs Aliu outside.

Flanky, Bukky and I joined Dongo to form a group. Dongo put the pearls around her long thin neck, and we all told her that she looked beautiful – in Yoruba!

After the school day had ended, we made our way back to Nile House, repeating all the vibrant Yoruba words we had learnt.

'*Sòkòtò* is my favourite!' Bukky said.

'And it shall be my new insult for anyone who gets on my nerves,' Gemini added.

'It means trousers! Gemini, you cannot call someone trousers,' Bukky insisted.

'But in America we say pants and I can definitely call someone pants.'

That made us snigger really hard as we made our way up the Nile House stairs; even Dongo giggled a little. Was she turning a corner? I felt happy about that.

Our mirth did not last because at the entrance

doors to the dorms we met Senior Moradeke and Ngozi, checking each girl before they could go in. There was a lot of noise coming from inside. What was the commotion about? I wondered.

Then the girl in front of us turned and whispered, 'Someone stole Senior Funmi's gold necklace!'

CHAPTER SEVEN
GUILTY UNTIL PROVED INNOCENT

After our school bags had been searched, we went inside and joined the other girls on the lawn. Someone said that Senior Funmi's mum had given the necklace to her when she died, to which another person said that they were family friends with Senior Funmi and they knew for a fact that her mum was still alive.

'Stop making up tall tales,' Tope said angrily. 'You're just making matters worse.'

'I bet it's fallen down someone's bed and it's not been stolen at all,' Caro said hopefully.

'Sometimes Caro, a bad thing has actually happened,' Lola said firmly.

‘Is it really pure gold? Why would someone bring that to school?’ Tayo asked.

That made everyone talk at once. I remembered seeing the necklace on Senior Funmi – it looked very special indeed.

Senior Moradeke stood on the raised corridors above the lawn and addressed us like old times.

‘Girls, we have searched everywhere for Funmi’s necklace. It’s a very special necklace given to her by her family.’

‘It was given to me by my grandma who just passed away, my sweet, sweet grandma!’ Senior Funmi began to weep bitterly. I had never seen her display any drama before; she was always so calm and collected. I knew this must have hurt her deeply.

We all stood there quietly.

‘How can we help?’ Tope offered.

‘There is nothing to be done, is there? We just have to wait for it to turn up.’ Senior Moradeke stood before us with folded arms.

‘Wait a minute.’ We all turned to face the speaker. It was Ola.

‘Didn’t I see you come back to the dorms today

after breakfast?' Her cold eyes were fixed on Dongo.

Dongo looked behind her to see what everyone was looking at. I could tell when she realized everyone was looking at her. Her eyes narrowed in disbelief.

'Walahi! You can search all my things, I am not a thief!' She threw her hands out in front of her.

'Then why did you come back to the dorm?' Ola demanded.

'I forgot my notebook! My notebook is very special to me too.' Dongo was defiant and bold. She didn't stop halfway like she normally did. I admired her boldness. That she would go back for her notebook made sense to me. I had hardly seen her without it.

'Hold on girls! There's no need for accusations,' Senior Moradeke said, trying to defuse the situation.

'We are going to the dining hall to study and we expect you to all keep looking until the necklace is found.' Senior Ngozi gazed at us sternly.

'But this isn't fair, we have to spend our evening . . .' Ola began to protest but then we heard a roaring sound of a vehicle outside.

'It's the fire truck!' Tayo exclaimed.

All of us looked to the seniors.

'Yes, go and fill your buckets. We will leave our buckets outside our rooms for filling. Please Tope, can you be in charge of that?' Senior Moradeke softened her tone.

Tope began to give girls the seniors' buckets, starting with room one girls of course.

'I will not fetch anyone's water until they say I am not a thief!' Dongo said it loud enough for all the seniors to hear as they left for their studying. She turned to us. 'Look how that girl made everyone start looking at me! Nobody stood up for me!'

'We are not used to talking back at the seniors but we can talk to them later,' Caro tried.

'I don't want a private apology for public disgrace.'

Dongo was like a dog with a bone, she would not let it go. This reminded me of the Dongo who got the ice lollies for me, the one who didn't let the Atlantic Four intimidate her. I liked this Dongo!

*

Outside the dorms, Chief Ogunbanjo was talking to some of the girls while another fire officer had already begun to fill buckets. The truck and hose made a huge racket, and the water spilt as the officer moved the hose from one bucket to another.

'He is wasting water,' Tayo muttered.

'Girl, just be grateful we get water today,' Gemini said, jiggling her waist. 'I need a whole bucket to clean this body!'

That worked. Tayo began to smile.

The fire officer was so quick with his job that Nile House buckets were full in no time at all.

'Well done Nile House, that was quick and efficient!' said the chief. 'Can someone let Zambezi House know it's time for them to bring their buckets.'

'Gemini and Jumoke, please go and let Zambezi know.' Tope turned to us.

'Gosh, who died and made Tope the oga of everyone?' Gemini said as we walked towards Zambezi House.

I laughed. 'Well, someone has to do it and she is room captain.'

'Yes, room captain, not house captain. All Form Three girls are in charge, not just Tope.' Gemini was tapping the side of her thigh. I knew that this meant she was losing her patience.

'Maybe there will be some benefits since we are in her room.'

'I guess.' Gemini didn't seem convinced.

The newly planted hibiscus bush danced in the wind as we walked through the front doors of Zambezi House.

Gemini announced from the porch, 'Zambezi House girls, it's your turn to fetch water, the fire truck is here!'

You could hear buckets being pulled from under beds and the girls started to come out of their rooms.

Rashidat and Chichi met us as we were leaving Zambezi House.

'Hey, what was going on in Nile House after lunch?' Rashidat asked, tucking her hijab behind her ears.

'What did you hear?' Gemini answered back.

Chichi lowered her voice to less than a whisper. 'We heard someone has sticky fingers at Nile House!'

I gasped.

'Y'all are crazy fast at listening to and spreading bad news. Who told you that?' Gemini said.

'Well? Is it true? And who is it?' Rashidat insisted.

'A more important question would be, how do you girls know something that only happened minutes ago in Nile House?'

'Nice try Gemini! Trying to change the topic. Tell us who stole what from who?' Rashidat was defiant.

'I know who it must be. Nothing was stolen before this term so . . .' A mischievous smile appeared on Chichi's lips and I knew what she was getting at.

'You don't know anything at all! Just mind your own business,' I barked at them angrily. I was so mad.

We walked quickly back to Nile House. I wondered who had managed to tell them so quickly. We had barely had the chance to digest what had happened earlier.

There were only three buckets left on the side of our dorm when we got back. Ola came to collect one of them. My orange bucket and Gemini's giant blue bucket were the other two.

'So you may have a thief in your precious room one club,' Ola said, following us.

'Stop being a troublemaker,' Gemini snapped.

In the hallway, Ola dropped her bucket of water outside our room and came in uninvited. Bukky and Flanky were with Caro trying to make Dongo forget the whole thing by suggesting she try on her new River School uniform. When she saw Ola, she rose to her feet.

'What do you want, Ola?' Tope hissed.

'Can't I come and have a chat with my classmate?'

Dongo huffed and pulled her white dress over her head. As she did, something fell out in front of all of us.

It was Mrs Kolawole's black pearls. Each pearl stared back at us accusingly.

Ola gasped loudly. We all did.

All eyes were on Dongo for the second time

that afternoon.

'I forgot to put them . . . Oh what's the point?' Dongo flopped her arms up and down, and ran from the room.

CHAPTER EIGHT
ALL FOR ONE

Nobody could say a word for a few minutes after Dongo left the room. It was Caro that broke the silence.

'Why did she keep Mrs Kolawole's pearls?' She sat on Dongo's bed with her head in her hands as if someone had died.

'Mrs Kolawole's pearls?' Ola's eyes prowled about as if this was some juicy piece of information.

'How did she get hold of them?' Tope asked, her brows very creased.

'We were allowed to work with them and Dongo put them on, but then she must have forgotten to take them off.' I bit my lip thoughtfully.

‘Or she hid them so Mrs Kolawole wouldn’t know she had them?’ Tope suggested.

‘Yes, but that was because she wasn’t supposed to be wearing them, we were just meant to discuss the Yoruba names for the items.’ Caro tried to explain to Tope.

‘Ah, I see,’ Tope said, her face showing a bit of relief.

‘But if she could keep these pearls, maybe that’s how she kept Senior Funmi’s necklace also,’ Ola said slyly.

Gemini had been quiet so far which was very unlike her. She gave Tope a look.

‘Ola, I think this is a matter for room one girls only,’ Tope said, nodding slowly.

‘I have a right to find out if there’s someone with sticky fingers in my dorm.’ Ola did not move an inch.

‘Hmm.’ Gemini’s eyes narrowed intensely. ‘I really think it’s time for you to go to your room, Ola.’ Her cornrows had come undone and she looked like a wild child who should not be trifled with.

Ola knew better than to protest this time. She

simply turned and left the room.

'I don't know!' Gemini continued speaking. 'I mean sure she's weird, but she just doesn't strike me as a thief.'

'She's not weird,' I offered.

Gemini laughed. 'That's because you're weird too.'

'Hey!' I protested.

A bright light pierced through the evening sky and all of us stopped for a moment to stare outside. Was that lightning?

'I agree with Gemini!' Caro spoke into the silence. 'Also, I would feel so bad if it turned out she wasn't a thief. I mean, if one of you were accused of something, I'd stick my neck out and say you were innocent until there was proof, real proof.'

A fierce crashing sound of thunder filled the room.

'Yes! Whatever you say, thunder woman!' Gemini said, making us all crack up as the rain began to pour down again.

Through the rain, we could see a tall lanky figure standing outside.

Caro cried, 'It's Dongo!'

Another streak of lightning splashed across the sky and we saw that Caro was right.

'What's she trying to do? Get herself killed?' Gemini said, but Caro had already dashed out of the room and all of us instinctively followed her into the rain.

'Dongo!' Caro shouted.

Dongo turned to face us.

'Come inside, you will catch a cold,' Tope said, wrapping her arms around her own body.

'Mosquitoes will bite you,' I added.

'Or a scorpion!' Gemini made us all jump with that one.

'Do you know lightning can strike us all dead?' Caro said dramatically.

'I don't want to go back inside, everybody thinks I'm a thief!' Dongo looked so distraught standing in the pouring rain like that.

'We have decided that you are not a thief,' Caro said.

'Can we just get out of this awful rain?' Gemini begged.

'Yes, let's get back inside,' I said in agreement.

I was soaked right down to my pants and we all looked a right mess.

'Nobody has oily fingers in our room or whatever that girl said,' Caro said.

'Caro, you are so funny. It's sticky fingers,' I said fondly.

Gemini looked at me meaningfully. 'Not many people use that phrase, you know?'

I nodded knowingly. Maybe it was Ola who told the Zambezi House girls about the theft. Maybe that was why she was hanging around us all of a sudden. Maybe Ola was one big gossip.

CHAPTER NINE
SHINE-SHINE RIVER

Several of us made our way to the Shine-Shine River on a bright windy morning. My eyes were wet from the winds, but it was the juicy egg rolls and mugs of hot cocoa that were responsible for the silence between us. Mama Tea had plastered the butter in between the rolls generously and chunky bits of boiled eggs peeked out of the soft rolls. It was so delicious. I tried to make it last for the whole journey but alas all good things must come to an end. I washed down the last morsel with my hot drink and cleaned my greasy hands on my uniform.

'I can't wait to see it up close,' I said looking at

Tayo. It had been her idea that we leave the dining hall and head to the river.

'It would be great to see if the rain has helped the river. It was sad to see it looking so horrible when we got back from the hols,' Tayo said.

'Yes, so many people in Lagos told me, it was the most beautiful river in southern Nigeria but when we crossed the bridge, the smell . . . erm . . . it . . . erm . . . well, it was bad!' Dongo blurted out, still enjoying the last bits of her egg roll. She seemed to be in much better spirits this morning. I was glad we had stuck by her.

Only Caro laughed. I suspect she was trying to soften Dongo's words. Most of us gasped disapprovingly.

'Ahn ahn, but it wasn't that bad,' Lola said.

'But she is right, it was horrid!' Tayo insisted.

Shine-Shine River was our pride and joy. It didn't pass around Kingswill College, just our school. It always seemed to shine in the sun and it was the source of water for us, Redbrick Bakery and the nearby town where most of the bakery workers lived.

As soon as we crossed the tarred road that

separated the classrooms from the red sandy hills, the smell that had greeted us on the bridge met us again. I held my stomach and looked at Tayo. She took off her glasses as if that would help her in some way.

'I may be mistaken but I think it smells worse than from the bridge,' Lola said, shaking her head.

'We would have never called it shine, shine anything if this is what it smelt like before,' Bukky said with so much despair, my heart seemed to give way.

'What shall we do?' Caro asked, looking at everyone, her voice shaking with emotion.

'I don't understand. What could be causing this? It can't be the heat. Last year was so much hotter than this and it smelt just fine.' Tayo was trying so hard to figure it out.

'What about the canoe race!' I asked.

'There's no way anyone can canoe in whatever is causing that stench.' Gemini turned to all of us covering her nose with her hand.

'You were right Dongo, it is dreadful!' Lola agreed.

'Wait, hold on a minute! What's happening? Yesterday you girls stood by me. Someone you barely know. And now you want to give up on what I hear is the best thing about this school?' Dongo looked at us all, her eyes compelling us with hope.

'But what can we do?' Caro held out her arms and repeated her question desperately.

'I used to live by the River Niger and that's the longest river in the country. We used to ride canoes on it all the time until my father died.' Dongo looked into the distance and then she bent her head.

Caro put her hand on Dongo's shoulder. Dongo turned to look at her before continuing.

'My father was great at making and fixing canoes. Then he fell ill and he was never the same again. When he died, his brother's family came and stole all his things, his canoes, tools, everything. They said it was tradition for the brother to get all his things, but I call it stealing. My father's brother is a thief! My mother could not fight him. When things got really bad, my mother sent me to Lagos to live with her sister and her kind family.

They sent me here. My auntie said I would love it because of the river.'

She had all our attention. My heart went out to her. I moved closer to her. All of us did the same.

'Then we must make sure you see the Shine-Shine River in all of its glory!' I blurted out passionately.

Tayo's eyes were darting around behind her thick oval glasses, as if she was thinking hard, but it was Flanky who offered a suggestion.

'What if my dad and Princey put their heads together?'

'Yes! If both schools work together, perhaps something can be done to save the river.' Tayo was getting very excited.

'Like what though? What can human beings do?' Lola asked.

'I bet you that human beings caused the problem in the first place,' Tayo said.

'Don't be so cynical,' Lola challenged.

'I'm not being cynical, I'm being pragmatic!' Tayo snapped back and we all joined in, picking a side and talking all at once.

'Big, big grammar that can't solve problems.

No water, no nothing!' Caro said quietly.

We stopped arguing when we heard what Caro said because we knew her words were true. If there was no water, then there'd be no corn, no canoe race. No nothing indeed.

CHAPTER TEN
SEEDS OF GREATNESS

It was the weekend and Mrs Aliu's voice calling us outside came piercing through the dorms. Everyone began to shift from whatever they were doing.

Gemini had been removing everything from her locker, from cookies to hand lotion. She had been planning to do some tidying but she was now throwing everything back into her locker in a panic.

Caro was folding her laundry. She had washed all her clothes with rainwater that she and Dongo had collected in their buckets. They even helped me wash my housewear with the promise that I'd help them on my next washing day.

Dongo, who had been scribbling fiercely in her tattered notebook all afternoon, got off her bed and got her tools from under the bed.

Tope was venturing into new types of novels. Gone were the riveting romances of last term with their dishevelled damsels in distress, and in their place was everything that had a crime to solve. Unlike the rest of us who seemed irritated at being interrupted, Tope tossed her mystery novel aside and jumped off her bed with enough enthusiasm for all of us.

'Time for planting!' she cried.

At the back of Nile House, Mrs Aliu was already surrounded by several girls and Mrs Kolawole was beside her. It was the first time I had seen either teacher in anything but kaftans and bubus. They both wore dark trousers and rain boots.

'OK girls, enough noise. Open your ears and listen to Mrs Kolawole, she has a small farm at the back of her cottage so she knows a thing or two about planting corn.' Mrs Aliu's voice was at its highest pitch.

'Good afternoon, ladies!' Mrs Kolawole's deep

voice commanded our attention.

'Good afternoon, Ma!' we all chimed.

'Today, I will be showing both Nile and Zambezi Houses how to plant corn. Behind your clothes line, a piece of land has been cleared for all houses.'

I had never ventured beyond the clothes line. It was just bush and we had been warned about snakes and scorpions, so nobody went there.

Mrs Kolawole continued to speak above the chatter. She was now on the move and speaking louder as she walked.

'You will create three long ridges, one each for Forms One to Three, and each form group will be responsible for their own ridge. Do you understand?'

'Yes, Mrs Kolawole,' we answered. Someone replied in a mock deep voice and Mrs Aliu eyed us coolly. Caro and Bukky had to use their hands to stop their mouths from exploding into laughter.

We followed the two teachers through the pathway between the clothes lines. Orange check dresses and bedspreads adorned either side and the smell of washing detergent filled the air. A wet piece of cloth slapped my cheek as the wind blew it.

At the end of the clothes line a large expanse of rich dark-brown soil lay before us. The smell of cow dung hit our noses.

'That's both rotten and rich!' Gemini was quick to announce what we were all thinking.

'Yes. We have mixed in rich manure for you so that you can have good soil to work with. Divide yourself into forms and stand beside a ridge. This one here can be for Form One,' Mrs Kolawole said, pointing to the long line of soil in front of her.

'Oya oya, Form Two girls, this one can be yours,' Mrs Aliu said, and the Form Three girls went towards the next long ridge.

There were over twenty of us in Form One and we all hovered around Mrs Kolawole as she removed the hoe from her shoulder and bent down to dig.

'You will need to build a mound all along your ridge like this.' She spread her feet on either side of the ridge and began to heap the dark rich soil on to it.

'I know how to do it, Ma!' Caro cried out.

'OK, show me.' Mrs Kolawole looked impressed already.

'Dongo, come and help me.' Caro nudged her.

She and Dongo tucked their orange housewear into the shorts they were wearing underneath and began to dig up the soil.

Gbish! Gbam! It was like a synchronized dance. Without looking at each other, they both moved seamlessly and to the same rhythm as their hoes hit the soft soil.

'Ahn ahn, Mrs Aliu! It looks like your house can win with these two girls alone,' Mrs Kolawole called.

'Ehn ehn! Wonders shall never cease! Look at these two!' Mrs Aliu was just as impressed as we all were. 'What are you all waiting for? Come on, join them. You have no excuse now, Form One girls. Get going.'

I jumped to my feet, fuelled by the expertise of Caro and Dongo, and started to build my section. The length of the ridge had been measured out perfectly so that each Form One girl had a portion.

After only a short while, Caro was done with

her portion and was almost digging into mine.

'This is very good. At home, I'd have to dig almost all this alone,' Caro said wiping her brow.

'I have finished already. Let's go and help others.' Dongo was swinging her hoe in different directions.

'Careful with that, Dongo. You will break someone's head o.' Caro laughed.

'Well start with me then. I need all the help I can get.' I winked at them and pointed to the mounds I had been building.

'*Kai!* Your mounds are too small, fa.' Dongo began to show me how it was done and the three of us continued to work on my portion of the ridge.

'Ola, come over and help us.' I recognized the voice of Yinka, the leader of the so-called Atlantic Four.

'See your best friend dishing out orders,' Bukky said as Ola crossed over to the Zambezi side.

'Hey, grow some loyalty,' said Tope. 'You're not allowed to go to another house and help them.'

'She can do whatever she likes!' Yinka snarled.

'Ola, can't you speak for yourself?' Tope wasn't

about to be silenced.

'Yes Ola, speak up and let them know where your loyalties lie,' Yinka said, twirling her cutlass in the air. Only a person who had no intention of working brought a cutlass to plant seeds, I thought to myself.

'I have done some of my section, what's wrong with helping my friends?' Ola still looked unsure as she joined the Atlantic Four. All four of them were wearing red bandanas.

I had to admit, Yinka looked very intimidating.

'Zambezi's going to blow Nile House out of the water with our corn and Ola knows it.' Yinka grinned.

'When you come back to your senses Ola, let me know.' Tope shook her head.

I don't know how we always came up with a suitable song but someone started singing and we all joined in.

These Nile House girls can raise a mound
Dùn dùn pá, dùn dùn pá
When it comes to planting, don't make a sound
Ssssshhhh!

We lifted our fingers to our mouths to silence our opponents.

Gemini stuck her backside in the air and began to work on her section in an exaggerated manner. We giggled so hard my ribs hurt.

CHAPTER ELEVEN
FUN AND GAMES

After spending the early afternoon planting corn seeds and fetching water from the fire truck, we were almost too tired to go out for games. But the promise of finally trying some canoe activities enticed us.

We removed our soil-drenched orange house dresses which we had been wearing over our games outfits and walked all the way to the river. I was in a large, mixed group with girls from my room and across Nile and Zambezi Houses. We had been the first to finish planting our corn. All of us were in white plimsolls and skorts and T-shirts with different-coloured crew necks. Dongo's long legs stretched out in front of me, a sack of skipping ropes hanging over her shoulder. Caro was next to her carrying a bag of board games. Beside me were Tayo, Michelle and Gemini. Tope was at the back with a host of Form Three girls.

We took the shorter way avoiding the dining hall and cut through the pond. The sound of toads and crickets filled the air and it was tempting to just stay there. Even though the pond was stagnant and carpeted by algae, it didn't smell bad like the river and it was surrounded by tall trees that made the air so much cooler than in the rest of the school. But the playground near the river was where all the action had been promised so we quickened our steps.

When we got to the top of the red hills, we all looked down at the Shine-Shine River. The smell hung like a cloak over it, but this time we were determined to look beyond that. Today, there was something much more exciting. Several canoes were sprawled out along the riverbank. To the left, a queue had formed outside the Redbrick Bakery van that sold delicious snacks on weekends and in the centre, several girls were already dancing, clapping and skipping along to popular games.

We grinned at one another, and we all knew what was coming next. We raced down the hills screaming and laughing all the way down. The wind blew through my afro and by the time I got to the bottom, I was so out of breath, I could hardly stand.

Ola was waiting for us at the bottom. Her hair was now gelled to its very tips and she had tied her sports top into a knot above her belly button.

'Chief Ogunbanjo has put the Atlantic Four in charge of activities. So if you have just arrived, please queue up for snacks, then go over to the games area until the chief calls your house.'

The rest of the Atlantic Four came to stand with Ola. They too had extremely gelled hair and tied-up T-shirts.

'So who is the chief going to call next? Zambezi, I expect?' I said, trying to sound as if I wasn't protesting.

'Zambezi of course, we got here first. We didn't use our planting time singing stupid chants.' Yinka raised one eyebrow.

'I don't have time for these creek freaks!' Gemini said and walked away towards the snack truck.

'We are not freaks and it's the Atlantic Ocean not a common creek!' Yinka balled her two hands into fists and stamped her foot on the ground. It was the first time I'd seen her lose her cool. I beamed at her before following Gemini.

'Gosh, she takes herself seriously. Creek freaks! I hope that sticks.' Bukky chuckled as we stood behind Gemini in the queue. Dongo and Caro were right in front of her.

I put my arm over Gemini and pinched Caro on her shoulder.

'Ow!' She turned to face us and broke into a smile. 'Have you seen the new slogan?'

The bakery van had a new sentence painted on its side. It said, '*Keeping your snacks fresher.*' The words were written in big red letters that seemed to bounce on top of the blue waves painted under it.

'Redbrick is really going all out with this new packaging of theirs,' I said.

'I certainly approve of those extra-crispy plantain chips,' Gemini said.

'Obviously the new owners have money. Maybe they can use it to freshen the smell of the river instead,' Tayo muttered.

The queue was really fast and Dongo was buying many packets of plantain chips ahead of us in no time.

When she turned round, she had several packets in her hand and offered them round. Several hands stretched forward including mine – it meant we no longer had to queue and I could hold on to my money.

When we got to the centre of the field, there were several games in full swing.

A few Form Three girls were already playing ten-ten. With rhythmic clapping and trying to match each other's leg positions, it was their favourite thing to play. But whenever the Form One girls tried to play, it became too noisy all of a sudden. So we had to be content with being spectators.

Caro and I had played it at home. Ten-ten was a very high-energy game and we loved it.

The aim of the game was to get through a round of clapping and counting to a hundred in tens without your opponent being able to guess and replicate the leg action you produced at the end of each play. I was too predictable and almost always pushed my left leg out on the first play and then alternate legs after that. As for Caro, nobody knew what she would do, ever! Ten-ten was a game of two teams with a first mother and a second mother. First mother got to choose her team members first. Sometimes it was just the two mothers against each other but when it was really exciting you could be as many as ten girls on each side.

One of the Zambezi girls shouted out to some others. 'If we get a big group, can we play Nile House versus Zambezi House?'

'I love ten-ten!' Caro immediately responded.

'I don't think she's talking to us,' I started to say but Caro was already running in the opposite direction. She approached the large group of girls in red. Ola was amongst them. Dongo's body stiffened as they all walked back towards us.

'I didn't see her there or else I wouldn't have gone to them,' Caro whispered to us on her return.

'It's fine.' Dongo shrugged and turned to play a game that had several other girls in a circle. I began to have a lot of respect for her ability to just walk away if she didn't like something.

Flanky and a few others were in the game Dongo chose and I wanted to join them but I also wanted to watch the ten-ten. I had no intention of playing it. I remembered the day Owolabi said I had the rhythm of a deaf mongoose when I cost us the game against the children that lived opposite us. To be honest, being a spectator was just as fun because the cheering and excitement until a group was declared the winner was utterly exhilarating.

'I'm first mother!' Yinka declared, suddenly appearing through the crowd that was forming. 'Who's going to be second mother?' She looked around fiercely.

We all started to look around too. My eyes met Caro's. The polite look I often saw on Caro's face had disappeared. In its place was a determined defiance she normally reserved for anyone who tried to harm her smaller siblings.

She stepped forward. A hush fell on the crowd.

Yinka eyed Caro up and down. 'Ha! This is

going to be as easy as shelling a groundnut!'

Chief Ogunbanjo walked towards us. Today she wore black trousers tucked into rain boots, a white polo top and black cap. She looked so different from all the adults that taught us. She was like an ally, a powerful big sister that knew things that we didn't. As soon as she opened her mouth, everyone turned to her.

'Well, I see you're just about to play a game of ten-ten. Let's make it interesting. Winner takes to the canoes first?'

There was a loud roar of approval across the playground and just like that the game of ten-ten became the game of focus.

'Ten-ten, ten-ten,' Caro belted out with quick hot claps that showed she meant business.

Yinka matched her rhythm clap for clap. She squinted at Caro, surprised at her efficiency of play. Caro refused to be distracted. They still had to go from ten, twenty, thirty, all the way to one hundred. Many girls from different houses started to move towards the Nile House side in support of this Form One girl with a mighty big clap.

As second mother, Caro had to try and mirror

Yinka's leg action three times in a row.

'Fifty! Fifty! Fifty!' they both cried along with us all who had become quite invested.

They both flung their legs forward, mirroring each other.

They went again. 'Fifty! Fifty! Fifty!'

Again, they mirrored each other. This time Caro's foot pushed against Yinka's foot. Most of the school was here now and everyone yelped.

The tension was palpable. If Caro could anticipate Yinka's next move and mirror her leg action on this third attempt, we would win.

'Fifty! Fifty! Fifty!' the whole school bellowed loudly. Some were even clapping in step with the players.

Caro pushed out a leg in step with the rhythm they had both been making, but Yinka held back for a heartbeat of a second and threw her other leg forward.

The crowd erupted.

'You hesitated!' Caro cried.

The crowd was divided. Most of the girls behind me agreed with me but the girls behind them were shaking their fingers. Girls like Bukky and Dongo who didn't understand the rules were very confused about what was causing the commotion.

Tope's and Gemini's voices were the loudest. 'Yinka don't lie, you know you delayed slightly in order to know which leg she would produce.'

Yinka had no choice but to concede. They had to go again.

Yinka did not give Caro another opportunity to come so close to winning again until they reached a hundred.

Caro's Cortina shoes were the very colour of dust.

'Hundred! Hundred! Hundred!' everybody practically yelled. Their hands must have been sore from all the clapping.

They both violently pushed forward their legs, producing a replica image.

The crowd roared. There were girls acting as informants to the less fortunate ones who couldn't get a good view from the back: 'They took the same leg.'

So they went again. 'Hundred! Hundred! Hundred!'

They both produced a mirror image again.

The crowd bellowed and everyone had now picked a side. There were just as many people on the Zambezi side as there were the Nile side. Nobody considered Caro a junior at this point. It was just two very skilled ten-ten players fighting for victory.

This was the last opportunity for Caro to take the victory from Yinka's hands.

'Hundred! Hundred! Hundred!' They clapped in sync along with the rest of the school. Just as they were about to produce their last leg, I noticed a slight distortion in the rhythm of the clap. Yinka was going to try her cheeky delay tactic again, but this time Caro pre-empted her and made a slight delay herself so that both of them produced their last leg at the same time. It was a perfect match!

Caro had won.

The crowd went wild and everyone started to chant:

Winner ooo Winner!
Winner ooo Winner!
Caro you don win o, Winner!
Pátápátá you go win for ever, Winner!

Nile House girls huddled around Caro and continued to sing and cheer. Yinka and her Atlantic followers were fuming. Ola, who should have been celebrating with Nile House, was giving me angry looks. They pushed into me as we walked past them, our orange polo necks flying high.

I sank both my hands into my pockets and looked around, but it just didn't seem like the right time to tell anyone that I thought my money had been stolen.

CHAPTER TWELVE
CANOES AT LAST

'Slow down, say that again, who bumped into you?' Tope said, trying to catch up with me.

I stopped for a mini second just before we ran towards the river. Tope put her hand on my shoulder.

'Ola bumped into me just after Caro won the ten ten.' I was trying to whisper because there were still so many girls about.

Game time was over and Nile House girls were heading to the bank of the river with the fire chief. The rest of the school had gone back to change and get ready for dinner.

'Are you sure your money didn't fall out of

your pocket?' Tope asked.

'Yes I am fairly sure. I kept checking until we bought plantain chips.' I stopped and bit my lip.

'So you bought something with your money?'

'No, I didn't need to. Dongo bought plantain chips for everybody.'

'What do you mean everybody?'

'I mean she bought for at least seven or eight of us.'

'Wow! That's a lot of money.' Tope looked at me as the thing she was thinking began to pass across my own mind as well. I shook it off.

'She has money like I have money.' I shrugged. 'There were several other people around me all afternoon.'

'I'd rather it just got lost to be honest,' Tope said.

'Don't tell anyone yet. Let me have a think.'

I squeezed through the crowd of girls to get to the front. The chief stood on a fallen tree log and was using her cap to dust off her khaki trousers. Barky, Princey's cat, pushed through and Michelle bent down to pick her up. Her black-and-white tail brushed past my face as she did so. It was now late afternoon and the sun shone somewhat humbly down on us, as if it knew its time was nearly up.

There were six wooden canoes and several wooden oars next to the chief.

'Good afternoon, girls. Today we are going to ignore the funky smell of the river and learn how to polish an old canoe. We may take one of the old ones by the water with some oars and practise how to sit and hold the oars. If you are able, you may even learn to stand without toppling the canoe over.'

She got down and grabbed one of the oars in her hand. She climbed back on to the log and stood tall and steady.

'What is your name?'

Dongo looked round to make sure it was her she was talking to.

'Yes, you. You are nearly as tall as I am. You'll make an excellent rower.'

'My name is Dongo,' she answered. And for the first time, I saw Dongo look really happy.

'Let's get started. Perhaps you can choose the Nile House canoe.'

Everyone watched on quietly as Dongo walked confidently towards the first canoe. She knelt down gently and shook the four panels that divided the canoe. Then she turned the canoe over with an ease that let us know she had done it before.

She shook her head and moved on to the next canoe.

'You have handled a canoe before, I see,' the chief said.

Dongo nodded as she seemed to reject the second canoe as well.

'Why don't you tell your house what you are doing?'

'Yes, Dongo, tell us, we want to learn!' It was Tayo that had spoken. There were very few situations where Tayo was not the expert. We moved closer.

Dongo cleared her throat and began to inspect the third canoe. 'The canoes are all very old but they are well made. I am looking to see if the seats are still sturdy enough or need replacing.' She turned it over. 'This is the best one so far.'

'Excellent choice!' Chief Ogunbanjo said.

'Does that mean we got the best one?' Gemini

pushed forward.

'Yes, I think you just might have picked the best one. What Dongo has done here is exceptional.' The chief walked over to the tree log and brought back a black metal trunk.

She opened it up to reveal many tools we had never seen before. Dongo knelt down beside her.

'Can I touch them, Ma? Back home, we use palm oil to polish the canoe because it doesn't harm the fish,' Dongo said.

'That's a very good idea. I will let Mr Lawanson know that we need some. Right, I will leave you here with a few girls while I take some other girls for a jog and some strengthening exercises. If we are going to learn how to row, then you must have good core and chest strength.' The chief raised her arms in the air and flexed her muscles.

'What of crocodiles?' Gemini said, looking around nervously.

'There are no crocodiles here now. They have all been tagged and removed by the wildlife association.' Chief Ogunbanjo sounded very sure.

'Ma, can't you row the canoe with Mr Lawanson?' Tayo asked.

There was a buzz of support and enthusiasm.

'There may already be a good candidate for that,' Chief Ogunbanjo tried to assure us. 'Besides, some of the villagers think it is a bad idea for a woman to ride a canoe.'

'Have they seen you?' I blurted out without thinking.

There were a few gasps and giggles.

'Jummy, Jummy.' Caro giggled the hardest.

'Sorry, Ma. I meant . . .'

'Actually, that's not a bad idea. Maybe I need to take the time out to visit them.'

Chief Ogunbanjo blew the whistle around her neck and began jogging. 'Who's coming for a gentle run along the river?'

Bukky and a few other girls groaned at the thought of any kind of sport but Flanky winked at me and we were the first to follow the chief. She was not jogging gently.

'Let's show this lot how it's done,' Flanky said to me.

It was funny how quickly you could get used to a bad smell. Jogging along the river was so peaceful as the sun fell further down the sky, but I couldn't shake the sadness I felt at how the stench took away from the specialness of this place.

We had only been running for a little bit and the Redbrick Bakery was just coming into view on the other side of the river, when we saw Baba Green's bus parked at the top of the red hills.

'Just the man I need to see.' The chief turned round to us. 'You're in charge of the jogging until I get back.' With that, she left the riverside and without stopping once, climbed up the red sandy hills. By the time she reached the top, Flanky was way ahead of me but the others were still way behind.

'Hey Flanky, wait for me,' I begged.

But Flanky was no longer running forward. She was running back towards me in a panic.

'Come and see, Jummy, it's dreadful.'

'What is it, Flanky?' I followed her for a few seconds and that's when I saw it.

Right there on the bank were fish flapping and tiny turtles trying to make their way back to the river. They were stranded. The river had receded terribly.

‘First it was the smell, then the water shortage and now this. There must be something very wrong,’ I said.

‘Definitely,’ Flanky said, her hands flopping to her sides hopelessly.

‘If it continues like this, there will be no canoe race,’ I said.

‘Let’s get the others,’ Flanky suggested.

We ran back to the other girls who were jogging very slowly.

‘Come at once! We need to save the fish and turtles. They’re everywhere,’ I yelled at them.

All of a sudden, Gemini had the feet of a gazelle. When she and the others saw the animals struggling, they were horrified.

‘Quick! Help the turtles on to their fronts and place them back into the river. Let’s try and save some of the fish that have not yet died,’ I said with an authority that surprised me.

‘Look at all these poor fish!’ Tayo was in a full flood of tears as she picked one up that didn’t move. She put it down and ran towards another. ‘This one is still alive.’ She ran towards the river and gently placed it there.

'It swam away, it swam away! We can still save some of them,' she cried, running to get as many as possible.

We all worked together to put the fish and turtles back into the river.

Caro picked up one of the turtles and stroked its bright green shell. It was so small and wriggled its legs and arms in different directions.

'Put it back now, Caro, this is not like your pet cockerel at home,' I joked. I could see she was getting attached.

Caro laughed and then bent and kissed the turtle's back. 'It doesn't look very well,' she said as she laid the little animal down.

I went off to help the other turtles.

'No!' Michelle cried as Barky who had been following her ran towards a flapping fish. She ran past Barky, picked up the fish and flung it into the river.

'I know what you were about to do, you silly cat.'

'Never mind Barky, look over there!' Tayo cried out in a panic. I looked up just in time to see a large eagle swoop down and try to grab one of the flapping fish.

Several of us ran along the river and shooed it away.

'Why are we shooing the eagle away? Who doesn't like free fish?' Tope asked.

'Something horrible is causing the animals to be stranded on the shore and it's making them easy prey for the larger birds,' Tayo answered, taking her glasses off and putting her hands on her hips.

'We most definitely can't have a canoe race on a river that is suffering like this.'

CHAPTER THIRTEEN
FROM ONE CHIEF TO ANOTHER

The noise at the assembly ground was like at a local market. Our assembly ground was a wide-open tarred space that could hold hundreds of cars when it wasn't being used for assembly. We waited for Princey and the teachers to appear at the top of the stairs that led to the staffrooms, where there was already a microphone and stand. Usually we lined up according to our forms but today we were told to stand in houses.

Senior Moradeke stood before us in full River School prefect regalia, her crisp white shirt tucked into her green skirt. She wore the green school beret with a River School crest reserved for outings. Her white socks slid nicely into brown leather shoes and her prefect badge that said 'Nile House Captain' shone brightly on top of her breast pocket. This was her final year and I would miss this impressive senior.

'What do you think they want to tell us?' Bukky said.

We were lined up according to height and as usual, she and I were the shortest two. I looked at the back of the line where I knew I would find Caro, Flanky and Dongo in that order. I hadn't seen Caro and Dongo this morning. They had woken up earlier than everyone and had disappeared from the dining hall straight after breakfast.

'Who knows? It must be something to do with the water. Today, I had to use half a cup of water to rinse my mouth and half a bucket to wash myself,' I replied.

'The Form Two girls came round to get two bowls of water from each person to water the corn. I bet that was Tayo's idea.'

Everyone started to turn towards the left of the assembly grounds. Bukky and I stretched to see but we couldn't. Teachers, smartly dressed, began to come out on to the opening at the top of the flight of stairs and there was now a quiet hum of voices.

'What's happening?' I asked. I heard the sound of a car door shutting.

'It's the new owner of Redbrick Bakery,' several voices whispered.

A man in a gold lace agbada that flowed to the ground mounted the stairs majestically. Baba only wore that kind of flowing attire when he was attending a wedding and even then it was never gold or anything so shiny. The new owner was a tall imposing figure and his brown shoes made creaky noises. With every step he climbed, he appeared taller and taller. His entourage of men and women in dark suits littered the steps beneath him. They each had lanyards around their necks and looked very officious indeed.

'Good morning, girls.' Princey wore a dark brown adire skirt and formal jacket with a shiny brooch on it. She had tied her hair up and looked so distinguished.

'Today, we are very grateful to the new owner

of Redbrick Bakery for coming to our school to see if they can help us address the water crisis and the troubling incident along the river this weekend.'

Bukky looked back at me and gave me a knowing look. I thought of the animals and wondered what would have happened if we had not been there to put them back into the river. My eyes must have conveyed my sadness because Bukky squeezed my hand.

'Redbrick Bakery and our school are the largest users of the river and so we will have to seriously reduce our use of water for now. Please welcome Mr Hassan, the new owner of Redbrick Bakery.'

Some people made an attempt at an applause, but it didn't gain momentum.

Mr Hassan adjusted the dangling sleeves of his gold agbada and took Princey's place at the microphone.

'Yes, if you want to applaud, do it confidently,' he said, grinning.

The teachers laughed awkwardly and began another applause and we joined in with some hesitation. There was something greasy about him. Perhaps it was his gold clothes or the way he crouched over the microphone that cast a shadow on our usually chirpy assembly.

'I am pleased to speak with you this morning. I want to assure you that Redbrick Bakery will do all it can to find out where the problem is coming from in your school.'

My mind began to race. Why did he assume the problem was coming from our school?

'We also want to assure you,' Mr Hassan went on, 'that this canoe race is the beginning of something special in our great state. We will be assisting the government in providing live music blasting from the factory and free snacks for all the spectators. As you will have noticed, we have gone to great lengths to improve our packaging and the taste of our products.'

He paused. 'You see, I myself am a rower and I will be racing for the north side.'

His entourage began to clap and soon a wild round of applause reverberated across the assembly. Mr Hassan grinned from ear to ear.

So this man had come to announce himself as our opponent. I didn't like him one bit, but everyone was applauding because of crispy plantain chips!

'In addition,' Mr Hassan said, throwing his hands in the air with great enthusiasm, 'I am opening up the Redbrick factory borehole and water tank for everyone at the River School to use! Together, I know we can make sure the canoe race takes place and Redbrick Bakery can continue to provide mouth-watering snacks for you all.'

There was another round of applause and some cheering.

I turned to the line beside us to find Tayo scowling. I was glad I was not the only one.

Princey took over. 'Thank you, Mr Hassan. That is very kind of you. Today, we will open up the path that leads from the dining hall to Redbrick Bakery so that you can fetch water at their borehole. You will be able to get both drinking water from the water tank to fill your kegs and bathing water from inside the borehole itself. If you use your water wisely, you may not need to do this daily.'

The reverend led us in a closing prayer and we were dismissed.

Five black cars drove out of the car park by the

assembly ground with Mr Hassan in one of them.

'How many cars does he need to come and talk to a bunch of secondary school girls?' Tayo asked.

'Don't you know that a convoy is the only way to get around?' said Yinka. Today, the hair of the Atlantic Four was tightly woven into six corn-rows and they synchronized their walk like soldiers. I had to hand it to them, they were immaculate.

'He just came to parade himself as our competition for the canoe race!' Tayo snapped.

'Exactly!' I agreed passionately.

'Do you think we can still win?' Tope sounded worried and I knew she was thinking of her dad.

'Yes! Mr Lawanson and the fire chief can do it!' I was getting very excited.

Everyone cheered in agreement.

'I wish we were going to the borehole with our class instead of our house,' Ola said, bringing the excitement down.

'Don't worry, we will find a way to get you in with Zambezi,' said Yinka.

It occurred to me then that I had never heard the other two followers speak. I didn't even know their names! I decided they would be Follower One and Follower Two.

'What I wanna know is, who's gonna go down into the borehole and bring the water out? Not me!' Gemini said.

'Isn't it so exciting?' Tope said. 'I have been in this school for three years and I have never been behind the dining hall. It's forbidden because sometimes the river overflows there.'

'That does sound exciting. Do you think it will be scary?' Bukky said, her eyes full of intrigue.

'Or perhaps there will be snakes and scorpions!' Gemini stuck out her tongue like a snake.

'But don't you see, Tope, don't you all see? It isn't exciting at all.' Tayo's eyes were filled with passion. 'If they didn't let us on the path because the river used to overflow, why are they now letting us go there? I'll tell you why! It's because it's now a stinking and dry river, drier than the Sahara Desert!'

CHAPTER FOURTEEN

IN DEEP WATER

Later that day Baba Green stood in front of the metal gates that led from the back of the dining hall. Seeing him there in his unchanging green kaftan reassured me that he would protect us from anything that dared to harm us on this wretched path.

'Good afternoon, Mr Lawanson,' Mrs Aliu said as she led us through the gates. Each of us greeted him as we passed with our buckets.

'Baba Green,' someone finally whispered loudly under their breath. I knew it was coming. Someone always felt the need, no matter how many times we saw him, to let him know we called him that.

'*Ẹ ṣá à ma rọra lọ*,' Mr Lawanson said, *Just mind how you go* – with undertones of *silly little children*.

Beyond the gates was a different world from the River School. The path was hard, and red and very dusty.

'This is exactly the kind of place snakes love to tread,' Gemini said, speeding up.

'I'm not even scared of snakes,' Caro responded.

'Neither am I,' Dongo added and the two of them walked ahead.

'Those two are as thick as thieves now,' Gemini said and regretted her choice of phrase as soon as she said it.

'I get what you mean.' I nodded.

'It's been such a strange term. Stinking water, missing gold chains and beads.' Gemini seemed unusually thoughtful.

'Caro and I returned the beads to Mrs Kolawole straight away. She hadn't even missed them,' I informed her.

'How do you like our new shiny owner at the bakery?' Tayo pushed in between us chirpily.

I was happy to see her in a better mood.

We were probably walking slowly and talking for too long because a queue had formed and Mrs Aliu was walking back. We put down our buckets to secure our spots and walked to the borehole. I had never seen one before, but I had heard about them from my grandmother in the village.

It was just as the name suggested: a hole bored in the ground with water in it. Its rectangular metal lid lay open and a Form Three girl came popping out with a bucket of water in her hands and handed it to the first person in the queue. She collected the empty bucket of the next girl in the queue and then disappeared down the hole again. The water in the bucket that had just been filled was pale brown as if someone had poured water into a dirty hot-chocolate mug. I consoled myself that the drinking water from the tank would be better.

'It's so dirty – must we wash ourselves?' I stared down the hole, only half joking.

'Phweet!' Gemini whistled. 'And it's a long walk back with a full bucket.'

'I wonder what's through there.' Tayo pointed

to the thick bushes covered in red dust ahead of us. 'Shall we have a look?'

Gemini and I looked around. Nobody batted an eyelid as we continued up the path that snaked round the bushes.

'It's really scary through here,' I said, half hoping that one of us had the common sense to turn back.

'Never mind scary, this has got to be the worst of the smell so far.' Gemini pinched her nose firmly.

With every step we took, the smell got more and more disgusting. When we turned the corner, we all pulled up our white inner tops over our noses.

'Oh wow,' Tayo said.

We could see Redbrick Bakery on the other side. Only a short bridge separated our school from the bakery. It wasn't like the beautiful bridge that led us over the river into our school. This one was old and neglected, with thick vegetation between it and our school.

'You better get any silly ideas out of your head, Tayo. I know that look of yours,' Gemini warned.

Before our very eyes, she began to follow the tiny path towards it.

'But what if it's dangerous in there?' I yelled after her.

'Yes, Tayo. We can't see what is ahead,' Gemini said but we were both moving forward too.

'We can't leave her to go all by herself,' I said, trying to convince myself that I had no choice in the matter.

The ground was beginning to change from rocky to damp. We came out on to a very small piece of shore. There was hardly space for the three of us and the river smelt like when the sinks in the dorms were clogged with stagnant water.

'Well, I hope you are satisfied now, Madam Tayo. The river has spoken, time to go back,' Gemini said.

'This looks more like trapped water, not a river!' Tayo snapped.

'Sssh!' I thought I heard something. We immediately retreated behind the bushes.

Two men appeared from the bushes on the other side. They were now on the very spot we had just been standing on. The way my heart was racing, I thought this must be what it was like to have a heart attack. I squeezed my arms around my chest to settle myself. Gemini and I bent down low but Tayo crouched over us. The prickly bushes pierced my arms and legs but there was nothing to be done. We could only pray the men didn't decide to walk this way.

The men started to speak and there was something familiar about one of the voices but I couldn't put my finger on it. I prised some bushes apart to see them better. One man was bald and considerably shorter than the other. He wore a dark safari suit that was too tight around the midsection. The taller man had his back to us. He wore dark, loose trousers and a polo shirt.

'So what will it cost for you to look the other way?' he said.

'Ah, it will cost plenty. You are using the river as a dustbin,' the bald man replied.

'Just keep your people from the bakery and I'll give you whatever you need. This should start you off nicely.' The tall man handed over a fat brown envelope.

The two men began to shake hands when

suddenly there was a rustling in the bushes we were peering through.

'What was that?' said the bald man.

I did not wait to find out what the rustling was – or whether the men were on their way over to us. I got up and ran as fast as my legs could carry me. I turned briefly to check that my two friends were right behind me and once I saw them, I ran even faster than I had ever run for Nile House.

Finally we came to the wider path and heard the sound of laughter and singing at the borehole.

We were all breathing very heavily.

'Remind me never to follow you anywhere, Tayo!' Gemini managed to get the words out. 'And you, Jummy. I knew you could run but your feet were actually touching the back of your head.'

I put my hands on my hips and laughed. 'I have never been more scared in all my life.'

'Who were those men and what were they talking about?' Tayo was not finding any of it funny.

You are using the river as a dustbin. I bit my lip.

'Exactly.' Tayo looked thoughtful. 'That would explain the stagnant water and the smell!'

'Well, whatever they were talking about is way bigger than the River School,' Gemini said seriously.

'The answer has to be over the bridge and I bet we can see more from the bakery,' said Tayo. 'We have to get in!'

She looked more certain than when she'd gone down the bushy path, and just like that I knew we would somehow find ourselves in that bakery.

CHAPTER FIFTEEN

CORN IN BLOOM

It was our room's turn to water the corn and remove any weeds on our ridges. We all went out early in the morning after doing our morning duties. We had used only half a bucket of water each to bathe so that we could use the other half to water the corn.

It was almost the middle of term and it had not rained for over a week now. The last girls who went out said the corn was doing well but the soil was dry and clumpy.

The sun was already settled in the sky when we got to the back of Nile House. We were in our complete school uniforms, and we didn't want them to get dirty so we walked gingerly through the clothes lines. Gemini and Tayo walked ahead of the rest of us with their hoes hanging over their shoulders and a bucket in their opposite hands.

Tope and I walked together. Dongo and Caro were nowhere to be seen. I wondered what they were up to.

'So you never found that money?' she asked.

'No. One minute it was with me and the next minute it wasn't.'

'We need to come up with a plan to get to the bottom of what happened to it.'

I had forgotten all about the money. As well as Senior Funmi's necklace. I wondered if Gemini and Tayo were talking about the men by the river and what they had said. We needed to come up with a plan for that too.

Our corn was looking very good indeed but it was true: the soil was dry and instead of the black rich soil we had seen the last time we planted, it was a dull grey. The corn stalks were already past my knees and some of the leaves were turning yellow.

We dropped our buckets and began to use our

hoes to dig up the ridge so that we could expose better soil. Then we went over the whole length of the ridge pouring water on the bed of corn.

'You girls come and see something,' Tope called from the Form Three section. 'Look at Zambezi House's corn and compare it to ours.' She stood pointing with her other hand on her hip.

We all walked over to stand on the path between both houses. The corn stalks on the Zambezi House patch were already at my waist and none of their leaves were turning yellow.

'But they planted after us,' Gemini complained.

'Yes but only by seconds, that's nothing in a corn's life,' Tayo said. 'Their soil looks as dry as ours, so it isn't because they have been watering it more than we have.'

'We should not be comparing our work with others',' I protested. 'Our corn is doing well.'

'But if we want to win, we must look at our opponents' work and ask questions,' Tope disagreed.

Just then, Dongo and Caro came running towards us in a panic from the direction of Nile House. Dongo whispered into Caro's ear.

‘It’s rude to whisper when other people are around,’ Gemini challenged them.

‘We’re not being rude. We had something to show you but we were not sure how you would react.’ Caro looked very upset. ‘Come with us.’

We followed Caro and Dongo towards the side of Nile House.

‘Let’s go and see what’s been making these two behave strangely all week,’ Gemini said behind me.

Caro and Dongo stopped beside an old plastic basin that was covered with a large wooden board. Caro crouched down low and uncovered the basin to reveal the contents of water and leaves. Besides that, it was empty. The rest of us looked at each other, confused.

Dongo shook her head and Caro began to cry.

‘It has disappeared. I told you it could escape,’ Caro said between sobs.

‘There’s no way that little animal could push over this big wooden board. Somebody has taken it,’ Dongo said.

‘What on earth are you both talking about?’ Gemini demanded.

‘We kept one of the baby turtles,’ Caro blurted

out in desperation.

We were still reeling from the shock of this revelation when we heard footsteps behind us. It was the Atlantic Four. They were smartly dressed in school uniform with the identical hairdos as usual.

'Lost something precious have we?' Yinka mocked.

'Tut tut tut! Room one girls, either losing something or stealing something.' Ola mirrored Yinka's exact stance.

'What are you doing out here?' Dongo advanced towards the four girls.

'Oh, we are not afraid of you.' Yinka stood with her arms crossed.

'What have you done with it?' Caro asked tearfully.

Yinka tapped her nose and smiled smugly. Then she turned and went into Zambezi House along with her three friends. Ola kept looking back at us.

'What were you thinking, Caro and Dongo?' Tayo was straight in once we were alone again. 'You took a sea animal from its home?'

‘Calm down, Tayo. It’s not as bad as all that,’ Tope said.

‘It is bad! Only God knows where those wretched girls have taken that poor animal.’

‘I just wanted to take care of it until I was sure it was better and then return it to the river,’ Caro tried to convince us.

‘Yes, we were going to return it today. We fed it with greens that we found growing at the back of the dining hall,’ Dongo said.

‘So that’s where you went!’ I had noticed the two of them sneaking off together.

‘Well I say we should get it back,’ Gemini intervened. I was so glad she said that.

‘Yes, I agree. And let’s remember, the river is polluted!’ I said. ‘So maybe, Caro saved the turtle?’

‘Look, it’s almost time for breakfast. We’ll meet at lunch to discuss what to do next.’ Tope was the voice of reason.

By the time we got back into Nile House, there was pandemonium. Senior Funmi and Senior Moradeke stood outside our bedroom with their arms folded, looking very serious. They shook their heads at us. The dorm was fairly quiet because several girls had already gone for breakfast. Others were dragging their feet hoping to find out what was going on.

'I know taking a poor turtle from the river is bad but boy do they look mad . . .' Gemini whispered behind me.

'All of you, come with us please.' Senior Moradeke was obviously trying to keep her cool but was failing miserably. Senior Funmi shook her head at Dongo in a most disapproving way.

'What have I done now?' Dongo said, following the senior girls inside our room.

'What could have happened in the last hour?' I asked.

'This is all my fault, not Dongo's. It was my idea to take the animal . . .' Caro was beside herself.

'Please be quiet, Caro, we don't know what you are talking about,' Senior Moradeke snapped.

Once we were all in the room, Senior Moradeke walked to Dongo's bed and picked up her pillow. 'Can you explain this?'

There, on an empty page in Dongo's notebook, lay a delicate gold chain with a heart on it.

We were stunned into silence for the second time in one morning.

'I don't know how that got there. Someone put it there while we were out,' Dongo said firmly.

All of us agreed and nodded.

'I don't know why you did what you did, but I'm glad to have my necklace back. I hope you will tell the truth now.' Senior Funmi looked up at Dongo.

'There is nothing to tell. I did not take that necklace.'

'Funmi, let's go.' Senior Moradeke stormed out with Senior Funmi in tow.

Dongo sat down on her bed. 'I hate this wretched school!' She put her head in her hands and wept bitterly.

CHAPTER SIXTEEN
FRIENDS INDEED

Nile House, room one was not the same since the day the seniors found the gold chain in Dongo's notebook. There was a horrible cloud hanging over our heads and I saw it mostly in Caro's and Dongo's eyes. This morning had started just the same. We were unusually polite to one another and nobody cracked any silly jokes. Tope did not boss anyone around, Tayo did not divulge any unnecessary stats and Gemini was as thoughtful as an angel. I hated it with every fibre of my being.

I went to water the garden with the water I had left over from bathing. Dongo was doing the same.

'Good morning, Dongo.'

'Nothing good about it,' she muttered without even looking at me.

'The sun is out and the birds are chirping away happily,' I tried again.

'I don't feel like talking,' Dongo replied and she poured the rest of the water from her bucket over the orange heliconia. They shook gently in response to the sudden downpour.

We heard the sound of an engine and turned to see Chief Ogunbanjo park and then jump down from her truck. She took off her black gloves and popped them into her back pocket.

'Good morning, girls.'

'Good morning, Chief.'

It looked like the morning might be a good one after all, I thought to myself.

'I am going into town today to take water to the residents. I think it is a good opportunity to introduce myself as you suggested, Jummy! The geography teacher is also taking some of the Form Three girls to see the effects of the water shortage on the townspeople. Would you like to come along?'

'Yes!' we both said without a doubt.

'Can we bring some friends?' Dongo asked.

I knew Dongo was thinking of Caro. How kind. I smiled at her.

'I have space for five back there.'

'What? You don't mean we will be able to ride in the fire truck, do you?' I was beaming from ear to ear.

'Yes, why not? I was just coming to get five random girls but then I bumped into you two. Let me know who the other three people are by first period so I can get the necessary permissions. We leave at noon.'

She put her gloves back on and jumped into her truck.

'Oh and dress really smart, the press will be there.' The chief shut the door and brought the truck back to life.

'You are a good person, Dongo,' I said, already thinking about how excited the room one girls would be. It was the very thing we needed right now.

It was all we could talk about at breakfast.

'It's a good thing I'm already going on the geography trip or I'd have been so jealous,' Tope said as she served us boiled yam slices and juicy scrambled eggs. She looked very smart in her full River School uniform, complete with a green beret which we only wore for external visits.

Gemini picked up her fork and pretended it was a microphone. 'Howdy ma'am, I'm from the American newspaper, the *Daily Bongafish*.'

I nearly wet myself. Caro laughed from the depth of her belly.

'You are a mess, Gemini!' she cried.

Later that morning, the English teacher had to send Caro out of class because she remembered the *Daily Bongafish* and randomly burst out laughing again.

We met the Atlantic Four coming out of the dining room after breakfast. They carried identical folders and all wore their green school berets.

'Hello, room one club girls. Guess what we had at our midnight feast last night?' Yinka said as she walked past us.

None of us answered.

'Pounded yam and turtle soup.' She tossed her head and Ola and Follower One and Two laughed loudly.

Caro and Dongo gasped in horror.

'I hear the missing jewellery has been found?' Yinka circled back and stared Dongo in the face. 'Hold on,' she said, suddenly eyeing us from our heads to our toes and saving us from answering, 'I know we're wearing berets because we are on a geography trip but why do you lot have berets on?'

Before I could stop myself, I said, 'Nile House, room one girls have been asked to accompany the chief in her fire truck into town today. We're going to talk to the press and everything.'

Yinka frowned deeply. 'Why should you be allowed to do that? Is it because Tope is Mr Lawanson's daughter?'

'No, Tope is going with the geography group just like you are,' I defended her.

'This is nonsense, why should we have a bunch of babies following us on our day out.' It was Ola's turn to protest.

Dongo did what we should have done from the start. She walked off and we followed her. I wanted to look back and see the looks on the faces of the Atlantic Four, but I didn't want to spoil it.

*

Noon could not come soon enough. The Form Three geography students were getting on the school coach and Tope stood at the end of the line so she could talk to us as we waited for the chief. We were so excited.

'I wish I could ride in the fire truck with you.' Tope sighed.

'I'm not gonna lie, I won't be thinking of you at all.' Gemini grinned.

Everybody's heads turned when we heard the fire truck revving its way up the assembly ground.

I clasped my hands together with glee and waited for the chief to dismount.

Just as we walked towards her, there was a loud thud.

'She's fainted, Ma! It must be the hot weather.' I recognized Yinka's voice.

The chief ran towards the crowd that had formed. In the middle of it, Ola was lying unconscious on the floor.

Mr Lawanson came running with a medical box. Mr Okocha, the geography teacher, got off the coach. The chief put something to Ola's nose and all of a sudden she sat up. Everyone cheered.

'We will have to take her to General Hospital in town,' said the chief.

I looked at my other room-mates. We all looked at Yinka and then at Ola who was now miraculously fine. I knew she was faking it, but there was nothing we could do. It would sound too mean to suggest it.

'Sorry girls, looks like I won't be able to take you into town,' the chief said as she lifted Ola up.

Without batting an eyelid Yinka and her two friends started getting on the coach. They didn't care about Ola at all.

'Actually, we're going to need one of her friends to come with us,' the chief added.

'Yinka is her best friend, it should be her.' Gemini was very quick to offer this piece of information.

'Yinka it is then, come with us.'

If looks could kill, Gemini would have been dead and buried.

'That means I have two spaces on the coach,' Mr Okocha said, looking at all five of us. 'Some of you already have permission, don't you?'

'Yes sir, these are the two that were originally meant to go on the trip,' Gemini said, pushing Dongo and me forward.

'Come on then, let's do some geography!'

Tayo shoved her pen and notebook into Dongo's hands. 'Take as many notes as possible.'

Tope gave the loudest cheer as we got on the coach. We waved at Caro, Gemini and Tayo who waved back at us with all their might.

My heart wanted to burst with love for those girls. They were the best friends in the world.

CHAPTER SEVENTEEN

OUT ON THE TOWN

The coach dropped us at the coach park. The sun was unrelenting as we walked in groups towards the square at the centre of town. I walked with Tope and Dongo. Mr Okocha and the two other teachers gave us bundles of flyers which we were to hand out. On the flyer was a picture of the Shine-Shine River as we knew it, lush and robust with Leke Leke perching together on its shores. There was a headline that said 'Water Crisis' and smaller pictures that showed what everyone could do to help.

It was a very busy market day in the square with many stalls selling meat, vegetables and fruits.

One had a sign saying there was no fish today.

The local TV station was in town too, interviewing the traders about how they were coping.

The woman being interviewed told the journalist in Yoruba that they were now used to the smell but that she could not leave her children to go and fetch water in the north side of the town, where some was available.

A few girls tried to get in the shot by standing behind the lady and making funny faces but Mr Okocha soon put a stop to that.

One of the other teachers took us further inside the market to buy snacks to refresh ourselves because we'd missed our break time in school, but then Tope said she was only trying to sweeten up the market sellers. It turned out to be true because as soon as we finished shopping, she let out a loud cry to get the traders' attention and then she began to speak in Yoruba. I got the gist of what she was saying. She told them that unless they reduced how much water they were using, the situation would get worse. She advised them to reuse the water they used to wash rice and vegetables for watering their farms and cleaning the fronts of their houses. She told them to bathe with a bucket of water, not under the shower. When she had finished, she told us to give out the flyers.

When we were done distributing flyers, we were split into three groups with a teacher each. We went knocking on doors – interviewing the residents about the effects of the water shortage on their lives and advising them on how to save water. Many of the residents were elderly or parents with small children who didn't go to school yet. They were very happy to see us. Sometimes the teacher did the talking, other times, the Form Three girls did. Tope was really good at it. She spoke Yoruba fluently and really connected with the people.

We spoke to one man who was washing his car with a hose. The water was flying everywhere. Tope put her foot on the hose and demanded he stop wasting water.

'Look at this small girl o,' the man began to protest. 'You can't tell me how much water I will use. Some other small boys from the other school came here and were telling us the same nonsense. Those ones even wanted to take a photo of me. I drove them away like I'm driving you away too.'

'Looks like Kingswill boys have been around today already,' I said to Tope.

When we returned to the town centre, we found some of them wearing 'Press Club' badges. I began to look around.

'Who are you looking for?' Dongo asked.

'My neighbour from home. He is a member of the press club.'

'Not just a member, but the editor of the junior magazine.' Owolabi jumped in front of me. 'I'd know that voice anywhere.'

'Hello, Owolabi,' I said, looking him up and down. He had a silver badge that proved his position as editor-in-chief. I was actually excited to see him but I couldn't very well show it.

'This is my friend Dongo and there's Tope over there. Her dad is riding the canoe for South Side.' I pointed proudly.

'Hello, Owolabi,' Dongo said, looking down at him and all his friends.

'Great to meet you, Dongo,' Owolabi said.

'Why are you wearing a blazer in this heat?' I asked.

'As an official of the press club, you must wear your school blazer once off the school premises.'

I looked at the other boys, who were not wearing blazers.

'They won't go far, these riff-raff,' Owolabi joked.

'You guys are not serious.' I laughed.

'Hey!' they protested, making us all laugh.

Tope came over when she heard us laughing. 'Hello! Share the joke.' She shook hands with Owolabi firmly.

'So, what brings your school into town?' Owolabi asked, looking around.

'The Form Three girls are here on a geography trip to see how the townspeople are coping with the water crisis. Dongo and I were supposed to come along with the South Side fire chief but at the last minute, she had an emergency.'

I scowled when I thought of Ola's fake emergency.

'We're kind of here for the same reasons. We wanted to get pictures to show the difference between how some people in the town are suffering and some others are not.'

'What do you mean? Do you mean like your school where there isn't any shortage?' I asked.

'We are beginning to feel the effects too because there is now more demand on our source of water, and so we too have to fetch water from a water tank that comes in every few days.'

'Oh,' Tope and I said at the same time.

'Some people don't seem to be affected at all. Mr Hassan, the new owner of the bakery, came to see us and tell us that there was no problem with our water. Did you know he's a rower? He's going to row for the North Side in the race.

'Anyway, we have been talking to the townspeople,' Owolabi continued, 'and according to many, there is something suspicious going on around the bakery. Mr Hassan has built a mansion behind the bakery with water fountains, man-made ponds and automatic sprinklers. There doesn't seem to be a water shortage there at all.'

'Come on, boys!' A short, bald man approached us. 'Let's get going.'

My heart nearly jumped out of my body. It was the bald man Gemini, Tayo and I had heard behind the bushes. I was sure of it.

'Wrap it up, boys. Meet me on the coach.' The man nodded at us and turned away.

I grabbed Owolabi and pulled him away from the others.

'What is it, Jumoke?' Owolabi was very confused.

'That man! I saw him behind some bushes at my school. He was talking to another man and agreeing to look the other way. He said the other man was turning the river into a dustbin, but he took an envelope from him. It might have been money! I am not sure what it all means but it is definitely something bad.' I was rushing all my words and my body was trembling.

Owolabi said, 'Well, that is Mr Eruku who works for the Water Authorities. He's come to the school to teach us about it.'

Mr Okocha too began to ask us to get back into the coach.

'I think you should take this.' Owolabi whisked me around and hurriedly dumped his camera into the bag I was carrying.

'What? Owolabi, this was your grandpa's. Are you sure?'

'Then do my grandpa proud. We were meant to go on a visit to the bakery, but it has been cancelled – I don't know why. It's up to you now. Get inside and find some concrete information about what's happening. There's something going on at Redbrick, I know it.'

My heart started to pound like it had behind the bushes. This time, it wasn't fear alone, it was love for my beloved Shine-Shine River. I looked at the sign that said, 'No fish'. I didn't know how I was going to do anything about it but I had to try.

'Leave it with me,' I said with all the passion I could muster.

'Ah I know that look,' Owoloabi laughed. 'Redbrick has entered hot soup.'

As the coach started to leave the town centre, I opened the camera bag that held Owolabi's precious camera. I could not remember ever being allowed to touch it, let alone borrow it. I pulled it out and something fell out of it. Dongo bent down to pick it up. She grinned and gave it to me.

It was a picture of me and Ola on the coach to school on that first day of term. I remembered that Kingswill boys had asked to take pictures of us and Ola had been sitting beside me. I looked at the picture again. Ola had her face squashed into mine, desperately trying to get into the photo.

'He must have taken another picture after he took one of all of us,' I said to Dongo who had not asked for an explanation.

'Or maybe he didn't take any other picture.' She smiled again, using her shoulder to hit mine. 'I like Owolabi. And so do you!'

CHAPTER EIGHTEEN
CREATURES OF THE NIGHT

It was late in the night when the frogs were croaking and the crickets were chirping and not a soul was supposed to be awake, that my eyes suddenly jolted open – mostly because it was so hot and humid. Then, I remembered Yinka's words about having turtle soup at their midnight feast. Where were the Atlantic Four most likely to have a feast? My feet hit the floor with determination.

'Gemini! Wake up,' I whispered. 'I think I know where the turtle is.'

My words were like magic. Caro was up in a second.

‘Dongo, Jummy has found the turtle,’ she whispered.

‘No, I haven’t but I think I know where it is.’ I was not doing very well with the whispering. Everyone was now awake.

‘Where do you think it is?’ Tope asked, putting on her torch.

‘In the box room!’ I replied, feeling very sure of myself.

There was a loud thud as Gemini got down from her bed.

In a few seconds, all six of us were tiptoeing on to the corridors towards the box room. The stars made pretty patterns over the lawn and the moon lay softly ahead. I pushed open the door of the box room and six torchlights scanned the room.

Our suitcases were neatly set in all the room’s four corners but there were four plastic buckets in a circle with pillows on top. You could still see the imprints of where someone had been sitting on the pillows.

‘Oh my goodness, Jummy, you are a genius! This is definitely where the Atlantic Four have been hanging out.' Gemini rubbed her hands together. 'The turtle must be here.'

We started looking in every corner of the box room but search as we did, we could not find the turtle.

'Jummy, wasn't there something you wanted to tell us when you got back from town yesterday?' Tayo reminded me.

'Yes! Tell us already – I'm tired of all this searching!' Gemini plonked herself on one of the buckets in the middle of the room but that was too much for the plastic, and Gemini came tumbling down followed by the pillow and the bucket itself.

'Oh Gemini, you are so silly, honestly,' I said chortling.

'Look!' Tayo was wild with excitement as she shone her torch on the water that had spilt from the bucket.

Scrambling out of the bucket was the most beautiful bright green baby turtle.

'Gemini, you found it!' Caro cried, bending down to pick up the beautiful creature. We all huddled up beside her.

I stroked the turtle as it lay tenderly in Caro's palm. It felt cold and hard to the touch. Its mouth gaped open and it crept up Caro's fingers with its small head moving as if it wanted to get to the light.

'Ooooh!' we all cooed.

'It likes the light!' Tayo said.

'Hold her.' Caro gave the turtle to me as she tried to get something from inside the wrapper tied around her waist. The turtle moved along my palm and its wet hard body tickled as it did so.

'I brought this with me.' Caro held up a wilted piece of spinach. She tore the leaf and fed it to the animal.

At first, it wouldn't even acknowledge that we were prodding it with a leaf. Then, it opened its mouth and held on to the spinach. Once it tasted the leaf, it just kept on munching.

'She loves it!' I cried.

'Yes, we fed it with spinach before,' Dongo said, stroking the turtle's back.

'What shall we call her?' Tope asked. We all looked at Caro.

'She really loves spinach so let's name her after

the most delicious meal in the whole school.' Caro beamed.

'We can't call her egg rolls.' Gemini's belly shook with laughter.

'I mean efo riro! Spinach soup. Let's call her Riro.'

I looked at the small creature with its green shell and yellow body.

'That's just perfect,' I said smiling.

'Riro. What a very suitable name,' Tayo agreed.

'We're going to be very tired in the morning,' Tope said, bringing us all back to our senses.

We all walked quietly back to our room, the turtle sitting gently in my cupped hands.

Caro dragged out the large rectangular bowl that she used to wash her clothes. It was full of water, stones and little leaves. Caro had never given up on finding Riro.

I put Riro inside the bowl and she took to it immediately. She swam towards its edges and we all cooed once again.

'Goodnight, Riro,' we all said one by one.

Caro put the bowl under the bed.

I slipped into my bed, excited about Riro and exhausted from all the happenings of the day. I still hadn't told the girls about meeting Mr Eruku and all that Owolabi had told me. That would have to keep till the morning.

CHAPTER NINETEEN
WE HAVE LIFT-OFF

If anyone had been looking at Nile House's room one table, they would have known something was different. We sat quietly at the table eating our meal of boiled yam and chunky corned beef with utter satisfaction. We had all played with Riro this morning, rubbing her belly with the toothbrush Tope used to brush her eyebrows. Tope claimed that since she was used to brushing her delicate brows, she should be the one to brush Riro the most. Tayo said she was sure she'd seen wild spinach growing around the clothes line and so Caro and I had gone to get some. She was right: we found plenty of purple flower spinach growing wild. Dongo had claimed the stones in the bowl were not enough and returned from her shower with sticks and rocks for Riro to rest on. Gemini left her torch on under Dongo's mattress so that Riro could get some light while we were in class. Nobody ever locked their room doors but that morning room one was locked.

I knew that every one of us was thinking of her, the beautiful creature who had come into our lives with her green shell and little bobbing head. There wasn't one of these girls I wasn't ready to tell anything. I leant into the table.

'The man we saw behind the bushes – Dongo and I came face to face with him in town.' I let the words roll out of me.

'What are you talking about?' Tope said, putting down her fork and looking clueless.

I looked at Tayo and Gemini. Both of them gave me a nod of approval and I told the whole table about the two men we had seen talking behind the bushes.

'Now this is getting very interesting,' Tayo said, pushing up her glasses.

‘We have to get inside that bakery!’

‘And I will talk to my dad!’ Tope said. ‘He might know Mr Eruku.’

‘Don’t get us into trouble. We were not supposed to be behind any bushes,’ Gemini reminded Tope.

‘But how do we get into the bakery? That seems hard.’ Dongo tapped the table with frustration.

‘What if we formed our own River School press club,’ I said, suddenly.

Tope jumped to her feet. ‘That is an exceptional idea. All in favour say yes.’

Everyone put their hand in the air.

I felt very chuffed with myself.

‘The beauty of a press club is that we can make formal requests of the teachers. We could say we are looking to do a piece on the bakery.’ Tayo pulled a pen from behind her ear and began to write.

‘Let’s say we are interested in how the factory works,’ Tope suggested, putting the last piece of yam on her plate into her mouth.

‘Yes, we can say we want to learn from their success. Play to their ego,’ I said.

'Wow!' Gemini said, her eyes shining with anticipation. 'Our very own *Bongafish Chronicles*!'

As we walked to class, Tayo began to draft a letter to Princey requesting the start of a press club. We all chipped in adding lines that we thought were necessary. I felt that we should go right in and say we wanted to visit the factory.

'I think we should save that for after we have been granted permission,' Tope said sensibly.

Caro agreed with her and so did Dongo. Gemini and Tayo felt the same way as I did and so we came to an impasse. We found a somewhat neutral party in Bukky who happened to be walking by with Flanky.

'Well, if the real reason for the press club is so that you can visit Redbrick Bakery, I'd say come out and request the visit right away. And what's the worst that could happen anyway?'

That seemed to bring everyone over to one side.

'We should show Princey that many girls want to join,' Caro suggested and all of us loved the idea.

So all day long, we went about recruiting girls

from different houses in between lessons, at break time and on every corridor. At the end of the school day, all six of us room one girls held the letter and put it through Princey's letter box.

'Well if thirty-three girls don't convince her, I don't know what will,' Tayo said, dusting off her hands and taking a bow.

The letter must have really impressed because we were the talk of the school after the next assembly, where Princey made more than one surprise announcement.

'I am so proud of the girls who have suggested that we start a press club at the River School,' she said. 'I cannot believe we haven't had one before now.'

She read out the names of all thirty-three founding members and announced us as the new River School press club to a loud round of applause from teachers and students alike. She went on to say that our first visit would be to the Redbrick Bakery where we would learn how the factory worked. She announced interested students could contact Tayo and Tope. Just before she dismissed us, she paused and smiled dramatically.

'Girls, I have one more announcement. It's about the canoe race.'

Bukky turned round to look at me. She looked worried but I knew that the look on Princey's face was not something to be anxious about. Mr Lawanson and Chief Ogunbanjo suddenly appeared through the group of teachers standing beside Princey. My heart rose within me. Could it be what I was thinking?

'Mr Lawanson and Chief Ogunbanjo will represent the South Side at the canoe race!' Princey announced and the whole school showed its approval by cheering, clapping and slapping each other's hands in the air. Many teachers put their hands on the two rowers' shoulders to show their support, and I put my hand on Bukky's shoulder too. This was the best news ever.

'I am sure they will do us proud!' Princey flashed her teeth at them.

The fire chief flexed both her arms which resulted in another round of applause and Mr Lawanson shook his head fondly.

'Enjoy the rest of your morning, girls!' Princey was still very excited as she dismissed us for the day.

On the way to our classes, more girls approached us wanting to join the press club. We collected donations from teachers and new members so that we could buy personalized press club accessories like badges, caps, notepads and pens. Michelle's mum, the French teacher, would help us get them from town.

Later that day, we asked members to stay behind after lunch to vote for the officials. Tayo was voted our president and Tope was press secretary. I was assistant press secretary, and I could not wait to tell Owolabi about it.

By the time the day for visiting Redbrick Bakery came round, everybody knew who the members of the press club were. Tayo stood at the entrance of the school bus and gave out press badges. She was already wearing her president badge.

'Jummy, here's yours. Press secretary,' Tayo said after digging through a black bag and producing several badges. There were two press secretary ones.

'Where's the assistant one?' I asked, looking confused.

'Oh I hope you don't mind, Michelle's *maman* said it would save money if it just said press secretary.'

'Mind? Not at all. I love it!' Now I really couldn't wait to show Owolabi my badge.

I put it on and immediately I started to feel very important indeed. I looked around. Even the non-officials had badges saying 'Press Club'. I could not imagine ever taking it off. I was going to wear it in the dining hall, to assembly and especially in the classroom so that every teacher would know I was an official of the River School press club.

The coach set off down the familiar path and up the bridge that led away from our school. This time, nobody waited for the smell of the river to hit our noses; we simply shut all the windows and didn't open them again until we turned on to a narrow winding road. As we opened the windows, the smell of freshly baked bread began to fill the air. The combination of the aroma from the bread and the galloping of the coach made me feel quite queasy.

Soon we reached the grandest golden gates I had ever seen. They parted immediately.

'See how the other half live?' Gemini whispered behind me.

As soon as the bus arrived in front of the factory, a group of security guards came to do a check of our belongings.

Mr Okocha and Mrs Kolawole, who were the staff accompanying us, led us out into the factory courtyard. Tayo was the one with the camera and when they got to her, one of the guards frowned.

'Not for use outside the factory building. Understood?'

Tayo nodded.

As we were about to enter the factory, we heard footsteps coming towards us. This person did not suffer from the embarrassment that normally follows when your shoes make such a sound. In school, the teachers skipped along the corridors humbly when their shoes made any noise that could disrupt lessons. This person approaching us had an I-don't-care attitude that made you stop in your tracks.

It was Mr Hassan, only this time he wasn't wearing elaborate gold clothes. He wore dark loose trousers and a polo top and was jingling a large bunch of keys.

I looked at Tayo and then at Gemini. We tried to look undisturbed by this imposing man but inside my heart was pounding.

He stretched out his hand to Mr Okocha and then to Mrs Kolawole.

'You have come to see how we do things at the new and improved Redbrick Bakery. None of that old stuff you used to put up with. It's all things new here at the bakery. Come, let me show you!'

And then he turned around to lead us into the bakery.

I gulped.

'It's him! He's the man we saw behind the—' I whispered to Gemini.

'Ssh!' Gemini clasped my hand in hers and we followed Mr Hassan into the factory.

Mr Hassan continued. 'Let me show you around our first-class facilities kitted with the latest engineering. We want the freshest groceries to be available to this town and your school. It's in with the new here at Redbrick Bakery.'

He took us through the whole factory, looking at how bread was baked on a large scale. He showed us the new machinery that they had purchased for the new packaging that kept their products fresher than before. After that, we walked outside through rows and rows of corn ridges much better than the ones we planted at the back of our dorms.

'Here, at Redbrick Bakery, we like to keep our customers totally and utterly satisfied. We are going to be the nation's largest producer of cereals. It's in with the new at the bakery,' Mr Hassan kept saying. Mrs Kolawole laughed every time he said it. It was very annoying.

When it was lunchtime, we went up a long set of stairs that led to a large hall with a huge balcony. We were served freshly baked meat pies and sausage rolls with a carton of juice each.

Each snack was carefully wrapped in the new packaging. It made a popping sound each time anyone opened a packet. The fresh taste of the pies nearly made me forget why we were here. Tayo did not forget.

'It's time!' She sounded irritated as she covered her ears from the sound of the popping packaging.

We joined Tope and Gemini on a balcony that overlooked most of the bakery grounds. There were strong winds blowing as we were so high up in the building. To the left was a huge estate of houses with a large selection of cars in different colours. A huge man-made lake sprawled out in front of the houses and a water fountain burst forth with an abundance that I hadn't seen since I left Lagos. Running round it all was Shine-Shine River as beautiful as ever, not even a whiff of a smell in the air.

'Look!' Gemini drew our attention towards her. She was pointing to a sign in the corner. It said 'No Trespassing'. The sign pointed to a stairway that led away from the balcony. It was sneakily tucked away to the side.

'That sign is begging for our trespassing!' Tayo whispered.

'Let's go,' Gemini said. The four of us climbed down the winding stairs. They were dusty and uneven, making for a very dangerous descent.

We made it without incident, and it led straight on to the type of sandy ground we were used to seeing around the shores of the Shine-Shine River. Leke Leke played happily on the shore, and you could tell this was home for the white egrets because they didn't even move at the sight of us.

We walked directly under the balcony so that nobody could see us. When we had walked past the factory, we were able to walk directly on the shore.

'It's funny how this part of the river doesn't smell and there are no struggling animals,' I said.

'That's the old bridge that we saw from the borehole,' Tayo called to us.

I recognized it. It looked as if it wasn't used by anyone but the bakery. There were several Redbrick trucks parked on it.

'Remember the stagnant water was on our side of the river,' Tayo said, courage in her eyes.

'So what?' Gemini said.

'Shouldn't we at least see if . . .'

'Don't tell me you want to climb the bridge.'

Tope looked very sceptical.

'What's the point of coming all the way here and not seeing anything?' Tayo pulled Owolabi's Polaroid from her bag.

'I have a bad feeling about this,' Tope said, but Tayo was already walking up the rusty metal stairs that led to the bridge and as usual Gemini and I were not far behind.

When we got to the top of the bridge, we watched to see if there was any movement inside the bakery vans. It was dead silent and we walked quietly past more than six vans all parked in a row. Once we were past the vans, the air began to turn sour. I followed my nose and looked over the bridge.

I gasped in horror.

'What is it?' Tayo ran to my side. Then Gemini and Topc.

A massive expanse of rubbish lay before us. It went on and on for kilometres and it smelt exactly like rotten eggs – just like the bridge closer to our school. Only this was the source of the smell and it was so much worse.

At first, none of us wanted to walk any further.

We didn't want it to break our hearts any more than they already were.

'This is dreadful!' Tayo could not believe her eyes. None of us could. She turned to look back at the bakery. Our eyes followed hers. Then we all turned to look at the other side of the bridge with all the rubbish.

'It's as different as night and day,' Tope said.

'And all the darkness is on our side of the river!' I said angrily.

'We've got to get a closer look,' Tayo said as she began her descent from the bridge towards the rubbish dump.

'Whatever happens, we stand together,' Tope declared, suddenly becoming brave.

'It sure does smell bad here.' Gemini was the last to follow.

Tayo handed Owolabi's camera to me.

When we got to the rubbish, our mouths hung open in shock. Every piece of rubbish was from the bakery, from plantain chips wrappers to bread wrappers. Even worse, there were hundreds of loaves of bread lying in the river that had now become stagnant. There were black birds and once white Leke Leke scavenging on mouldy food.

'Look! Take that picture, Jummy,' Tayo shrieked.

She was pointing to a large industrial fridge, rusty and abandoned in the middle of the mess. Half its body was submerged in stagnant water. I poised myself ready to take the photo. Just then a huge rat with the longest tail I had ever seen mounted the fridge just before I pressed the click button.

'Vermin!' Gemini whispered.

'Yes, that's what these people are!' Tope added.

Out came the photo with its white outline of images. I shook it vigorously the way I had seen Owolabi do many times and a clearer picture started to form.

'Excellent photo, Jummy!' Tayo said and then she bent down low and began to retch violently.

'Sorry Tayo, it does smell pretty bad,' Tope said, rubbing her back. I was still flapping the photo up and down.

'Did you see the size of that rat?' Gemini made an exaggerated show with her hands.

'It's not the smell or the rats,' Tayo began. 'I just

can't believe anyone would be so thoughtless and wasteful. There are people in the town that would give anything for some of this bread.'

'So this is what they did with the old packaging,' Tope said furiously. 'This is incredibly shocking! Please take more pictures, Jummy.'

I looked at the one in my hands. I handed it to Tayo.

'Wow! Jummy, that's a very good shot.'

'Get into some of the pictures so they know we were here, not in some rotten canal,' I said, feeling like quite the photographer. I got one with mouldy loaves of bread and one with the girls in front of the rubbish.

'I was closing my eyes in this one, let's take another,' Tope said, only joking a little.

'I think we better get back,' Tayo said. I handed the camera and pictures to her.

When we got back to the balcony, we tried to slip in unnoticed but Mr Okocha was too observant to let that go.

'You should have asked permission before you went out,' he said in his booming deep voice.

'Yes sir, we should have. We were so excited for

our newsletter and getting all the right details for our cover story.' Tayo sounded like a most proficient president.

'*Bongafish Chronicles*.' Gemini laughed at the ridiculousness of the name and so did we.

'Some of the best magazines have ridiculous names but that's what makes them memorable,' Mr Okocha said, surprising us.

Mr Hassan returned with another man who was carrying several red goody bags labelled 'Redbrick Bakery'.

'Thank you, sir.' Everyone sounded so excited when they received their bags.

There were several squeals of delight as girls started rummaging through them. This pleased Mr Hassan very much.

'We aim to please at Redbrick Bakery. Everything you have there is brand new. Never been seen or tasted before. It's in with the new at the bakery now,' he said for the umpteenth time that day.

Inside my goody bag was a small loaf of honey bread, a thermometer, a see-through pencil case with Redbrick Bakery stationery and a cool red cap.

Everything in the bag made me sick. Many girls put on the caps.

Tayo went round and told them to put their berets back on. She said it didn't go with our school uniforms but I knew she was feeling as sick as I was.

Our teachers thanked Mr Hassan and asked Tayo to say thank you on behalf of us all.

'Thank you, sir for your hospitality and tour of the bakery. We will dump all our rubbish notions about business and cling to all we have learnt here.' Tayo grinned cheekily.

All the adults looked at Tayo strangely. I looked over at Gemini and chuckled internally.

We said our goodbyes and got back on the coach.

As we approached the grand golden gates, a siren began to wail. The gates stayed closed.

Three long black cars appeared and surrounded us.

'What is going on?' Mr Okocha stood up and got off the bus.

A man came out from one of the cars and spoke with him. After a few moments, he came back on and said there had been some misunderstanding and that we had to come off the coach with all our things.

'I think it may be us,' Tayo said.

It had never occurred to me until that moment that the alarm was for us. Maybe they had seen us sneaking back from the bridge. My heart began to beat with pure unadulterated fear. Fear of being caught, being reported to Princey and potentially shutting down the press club before it even began.

The security guards did not search our bags as we thought they would. Instead, Mr Hassan emerged from the long black car in the middle of the two others.

He stepped forward and began to speak.

'I have provided you with access to my factory and some of you have decided to return the favour by snooping around the premises and venturing to unauthorized areas. Without wasting my time, will the four guilty parties step forward? I have video evidence here.' He spoke with so much self-importance that my emotions were shifting from fear to irritation and defiance. What was all this drama for?

'Sir, I am sure we can work this out—' Mrs Kolawole tried to intervene.

'Until the girls step forward, there will be no discussions,' Mr Hassan said.

Tayo looked at me and nodded. I looked at Gemini and Tope. I was annoyed and suddenly I didn't care what would happen. We all stepped forward at the same time.

'Now hand over the camera and pictures that you took illegally.'

Tayo's mouth dropped to the floor. She looked defeated for the first time since we started our press club activities. But she opened her bag and handed him all the pictures and the camera. He took the bag from her and checked to see if there were any more pictures left inside.

'Good! Maybe now you will go back to school and think about what you have done. I will be ringing your school principal immediately. You are free to go.' Mr Hassan got into his car and left us.

What started as an honourable trip as the prestigious press club ended with drooping heads and heavy hearts. Everyone was quiet and full of despair on the coach ride back to school. I couldn't shake the feeling of how fruitless the journey had been and the thought of what Princey would say made my heart sink even further.

CHAPTER TWENTY
FACING THE PRINCIPAL

Over the weekend, the rumours that followed our press club debut were relentless. First, someone said we had been asked to leave because the tour guide could not answer all Tayo's incessant questions. Another story was that Gemini had been rude to Mr Hassan himself and the most ridiculous of them all was that we had eaten the corn that was growing on the Redbrick Bakery farm and so we had to be dismissed.

'What utter nonsense!' Tope said, kissing her teeth as she got into her bed for siesta. We had all been playing with Riro before the siesta bell went. Dongo lay down on her bed with her head turned downwards to the floor and I wondered if she was still secretly playing with Riro, who was under her bed.

There was a knock on our room door and Ola walked in. There was a scowl on her face. She hadn't quite forgiven us for taking back our turtle and you could tell she was just looking for the right time to strike back.

She eyed Dongo who didn't give her the time of day.

'What do you want, Ola? Make it quick,' Gemini snapped at her.

'Mrs Aliu said that the four of you are wanted in Princey's cottage right now.' A small smile was dancing around her lips as she spoke.

Tope jumped off her bunk immediately, as did I.

'Wow! Summoned to the principal's house over the weekend, it must be serious.' Ola bit her bottom lip. 'If you let me see the turtle I might not tell anyone . . .' She raised her eyebrow and Dongo sat up and used her legs as a guard between Ola and the turtle. Ola shrugged and slammed our room door behind her on her way out.

Tope, Tayo, Gemini and I made our way

towards Princey's cottage. The beautifully manicured lawn and the orange heliconia made us feel welcome, but we were very nervous. I followed the girls up to the grey mosquito-net door. The wooden front door behind it was wide open.

Tayo looked back at us and knocked on the door. We heard the sound of footsteps coming towards us.

'Good afternoon. Come in, girls.' Princey's usual warmth was gone and in its place was a mixture of disappointment and sternness.

We looked at each other sad and terrified.

Then we followed Princey through a long white corridor with several doors. I had been here before but only to the kitchen to get snacks for the Nile House picnic many moons ago.

Princey led us into a beautifully decorated living room with a chocolate-brown sofa and four lounge chairs. There was a glass coffee table in the centre with several bottles of soft drinks and glasses on it.

The two teachers who had accompanied us on the trip, Mr Okocha and Mrs Kolawole, sat on lounge chairs. They did not smile at us when we entered the room. Mrs Aliu was there too and her eyes were filled with displeasure.

'Good afternoon, sir, good afternoon, Ma.' We all greeted the adults by curtseying. We were very fearful of what we had walked into.

Princey sat down too. 'Take a seat on the sofa,' she said.

We all fitted easily on the large sofa.

'So girls,' she went on, 'Mr Okocha has told me that you disappeared at some point during your visit to the bakery.'

He gave us a firm look but I thought I could detect a hint of mercy. Then he turned to look at Princey who began to speak again.

'Mr Hassan has also been on the phone to me and now I want to hear from you.'

Tope looked to Tayo who had hardly spoken a word since the incident.

'Ma, we wanted to get pictures for the press club and so we decided to look around,' Tayo said meekly. I looked up at her to see if she would say more but she didn't.

'Hm! Mr Okocha, what do you think?'

'I feel, Ma, that the girls were simply taking

their task as River School press club very seriously. They already have a name for their magazine. Eh girls, *Bongafish Chronicles*.'

Princey nearly smiled but that was cut short by Mrs Kolawole who shifted forward in her chair.

'Ma, it was very embarrassing. You know I am not one to be so serious, but this was disgraceful. We all had to come out and be paraded like common criminals. I even tried to appease the man, but he might as well have said I should shut up in front of the girls. Imagine?! Ah, it was very embarrassing o!' Mrs Kolawole's legs shook as she spoke and this made her whole body jiggle like jelly.

'We had heard rumours about the bakery and we wanted to investigate,' Tayo blurted out in our defence. We all looked at her – she had given the game away!

'You did not have permission to do that. You were meant to be looking at the factory and corn-fields only.' Mrs Kolawole snapped at us in irritation and Tayo, who had leant forward to speak, moved back into the sofa again.

'Mr Hassan said he wouldn't have minded but

that the bakery site is dangerous. He said you even went on an old bridge that is not in use any more. He was very concerned about your safety.' Princey looked at us with concern herself. 'Imagine if one of you had been hurt, what would I tell your families, ehn?'

We all looked at each other. I wished we had the pictures to show them but we had nothing.

'And listening to rumours is not what a press club is for. It's for truth and justice,' Princey added.

'That is what we were trying to do, Ma!' Tope exclaimed.

'That is enough now, girls. Mr Hassan feels there has to be some form of repercussion for loitering, so we have agreed that you will go back to the bakery and help with weeding and harvesting of their corn plantation. You will start on Monday after lunch for a few hours. I know you have end-of-year exams coming up soon and that is why I cut it down. Mr Hassan wanted you to do a week.' Princey looked at the other adults and then at us and smiled for the first time that afternoon.

'Thank you, Ma,' we said together.

With that, Princey stood up. 'Let me show you out,' she said, 'and please, no loitering while on the bakery premises this time. OK?'

'But Ma . . .' I turned to face Princey as we stepped on to the lawn.

'Yes, Jumoke Afolabi?'

'Are we still the River School press club?'

'Of course. What is a press club if it doesn't run into a little challenge from time to time.'

'But now we have no camera, Ma. Mr Hassan confiscated it.' The earnestness in Gemini's voice could have moved a mountain.

'All in due time, my girls, all in good time.'

Princey closed the net door and walked back inside. I stared after her for a while. I wish we had said more but I was also relieved that the punishment was not as severe as I thought. At least we were still the River School press club.

CHAPTER TWENTY-ONE
REBELS WITH A CAUSE

Rows and rows of corn higher than the ones we were planting behind our dorms spread out in front of us. There were several workers on the bakery site already. Some were pulling up weeds while others were harvesting corn and putting it into baskets.

'That rumour about us eating the corn on the farm may turn out to be some kind of prophecy,' Gemini joked.

A lady came to show us how to do the work and we got on it straight away.

I was the best out of the four of us because, as well as our practice at school, I had done this at home with Caro's family who harvested a few rows of corn and roasted them for the children in the compound.

'You can't just pull the weed like that,' the lady said to Gemini as she tried to speed through the work. 'If you do that, you will spoil the corn plant.'

'Yes Ma,' Gemini said politely as she tried to slow down.

'It's like this Ma, isn't it?' Tope said, a little too smugly.

'Well done, Madam Weed,' Gemini said sarcastically.

The lady threw her head back and laughed. 'You girls will do well here, you are hard-working and you know how to laugh.' She was a very skinny woman but when she bent her body back like that her tummy protruded in an awkward way.

'Oya, get to work. I will inspect what you have done before you leave.' She walked to another part of the farm to continue her own work.

One hour went by so fast. We had only filled one large basket with corn and a little basket with weeds, but the lady seemed happy with our work.

'Good girls,' she said. 'Very hard-working.'

When we had got into a steady routine, she let us work with her at the far end of the farm where the special-variety plants were.

All we had to do was switch on the sprinklers and they produced water in abundance.

'Look at how much water they have to do what they like, while some of us have to travel to a borehole,' Tayo hissed, meaner than a snake.

'Well, it is a ginormous farm.' Gemini spread her arms wide for emphasis.

'And they have ginormous corn. Look at this one.' Tope pointed to the largest cob of corn I had ever seen.

Suddenly, the sprinklers came on unexpectedly and splashed at us. Tope and I screamed and giggled.

'Yes! I did that so you will stop talking and get back to work.' Our supervisor wagged her finger at us.

We continued our work in silence until someone in the section next to ours spoke. We couldn't see her behind the tall corn stalks.

'So, I heard you girls tried to take pictures of

the bakery and got into trouble.'

We all stopped what we were doing but we didn't say a word.

'That picture you took of the rat on the fridge. That was a good one,' the person tried again and this time we walked towards where the voice was coming from.

Behind the tall corn, a girl was stretching her body and yawning loudly. 'I see that got your attention,' she said, winking at us cheekily.

'How do you know about that picture?' I quizzed her.

'I know everything that goes on here.' She extended her hand to us. 'I'm Segun and I go to the night school in town, but I work here in the daytime. I pick corn, load the trucks with bread and I clean nasty men's offices. Sometimes those nasty men leave telling pictures on their desks.' Segun was smiling and raising her eyebrows up and down.

We all gasped; mine was the loudest.

'I took those pictures!' I cried.

'They are very good. I wanted to take them as evidence because I have been telling my father about what Mr Hassan is doing but he doesn't believe me. He says I'm getting carried away with my education.'

'I wish you had taken them,' Tayo said wistfully.

'Mr Hassan came into the office and locked them in his drawer.'

'That man is as sly as they come,' Gemini said.

'If he was smart, he would have destroyed them,' Tayo said, looking around us. The lady who had been supervising us was nowhere to be seen.

'Are you thinking what I'm thinking?' Segun raised her brows again but this time to Tayo specifically. Tayo nodded vigorously.

'Oh you girls can't be serious. What are you thinking?' Tope said, throwing a cob of corn into a basket. I think she already knew the answer.

'This time you can't blame us. We were here minding our business when trouble came to find us.' Gemini threw her corn on the floor and began to follow Segun and Tayo.

'Tope, just think,' I said, 'if we get the pictures, Princey will understand why we did what we did.'

She shrugged and smiled. 'What was it Princey said? A press club is for truth and justice.'

Tope pushed her arm into mine and we followed the three girls.

'I live in town. My father is a fisherman, and we cannot catch or eat any fish. We are really struggling,' Segun was saying to Tayo and Gemini when we caught up.

I remembered the fish stall that was closed when we went into town.

'Don't we have to find out where Mr Hassan is before we start loitering again? And I think they have cameras!' Tope kept fluctuating between bravery and fear.

'That's easy, you'll soon see him just before we come out of the last row of corn.'

'What?' This time all of us froze.

'Don't worry, he won't see us.' Segun kept moving but now she was making sure she didn't make a sound. We did the same.

'Look,' Segun whispered and stopped behind the last row of corn. In between the stalks, I could see the lake we had seen from the balcony. There was someone on it rowing a canoe.

'That's your Mr Hassan. He'll be there for hours. Even if they catch you on camera, you'll be long gone. But make sure you show it to your head teacher immediately.'

'How far is the office from here?' Tayo looked at her watch.

'Five minutes tops,' Segun reassured us.

She led us to the end of the corn and up the forbidden stairs we had used on our last visit. When we got on to the balcony, I looked to make sure Mr Hassan was still on the lake. The canoe seemed to glide quickly and effortlessly through the water.

'Where is everyone?' Gemini asked.

'The office workers are having their break,' Segun said, quickening her steps as she led us down a dark corridor and then into a large office. She didn't turn on the lights but went straight towards the big desk at the back of the room. She tried the drawer. 'It's locked,' she said.

'Do you know where he keeps the key?' Gemini said.

'In one of these cabinets.'

That would have been a good answer if the entire office were not covered from ceiling to floor in cabinets.

'Ah, we should have asked her all these questions before we left.' Tope sounded both scared and irritated.

Tayo was at the desk with Segun and Gemini was looking around the office.

'I can't take this, I'm going to keep a lookout on the lake. If he gets out, I'll let you know.' Tope ran towards the balcony.

'That's actually a good idea,' I said after her.

I walked slowly around the room. Segun was opening and shutting all the wall cabinets. There was a picture of Mr Hassan rowing on the wall. Even in the darkness, I could see he had strong arms and a broad chest which looked excellent for a rowing champion. I gulped. I wasn't sure what the South Side could do against such a formidable fellow.

'Aha!' Segun said all of a sudden. 'I found it.' She was standing in front of one of the cabinets. Inside were various bunches of keys.

'Oh no! How on earth are we supposed to

know which one it is?' It was Gemini's turn to feel frustrated.

'It's this one!' Segun reached into the cabinet and picked one out. 'I remember this!' She pointed to a gold bar keyholder that shone in the dark.

She tried it in the lock of the desk and pulled open the top drawer but it only held envelopes and pens. She lifted up the envelopes. Nothing. My heart had started to pound viciously. She began to open the other drawers, one by one.

'This is taking too long,' Tayo was saying when I heaved a sigh of relief.

The camera and pictures were in the bottom drawer.

'We can't take the camera, can we?' I asked, even though I knew Owolabi would want me to.

'Take everything. He will probably think it was me because he caught me looking at them. I'll deny it or maybe I just won't come back here tomorrow.' Segun shrugged.

There was a sudden patter of running feet towards us. Tope rushed into the room.

'Quick, he has come out of his canoe. Quick!'

The panic in Tope's voice moved us into action.

I grabbed the camera. Tayo grabbed the photos. We ran out to the dark corridor and on to the balcony. We made sure we kept to the wall so that nobody could see us. I looked out on to the lake as we made our way off the balcony. Mr Hassan was no longer there. Just an empty canoe lay still on the lake. What if we met him on the stairs? Fear made my feet heavy as we climbed down step by step.

When we got to the bottom of the stairs, we made to go forward into the cornfields but stopped as we heard someone whistling a jolly tune.

Segun turned back immediately and led us behind the wall that led up the stairs. If I thought I had been scared behind those bushes at the bore-hole, this was a hundred times more intense. I thought I was going to vomit for the terror that was running through me.

Each of us lay flat against the wall. We could see the cornfields ahead but we dared not move. The whistling continued as the person mounted the stairs. It echoed long after their footsteps faded into the building.

‘Run!’ Segun said.

We ran as fast as we could to the safety of the cornfield. The wind was blowing into my face and the fear turned into exhilaration as we reached the section we had been working in. I quickly put the camera into my school bag.

‘Where have you been?’ our supervisor shouted at us.

‘I took them to the toilet,’ Segun said quickly.

‘You should have told me. Finish up, your school bus should be arriving any minute now.’

Tayo turned to Segun. ‘Thank you so much!’

‘No, thank you! I would not have been so brave without you all.’

Tayo took out the pictures from her pocket and showed one of them to us. It was of the old bridge and the rubbish flowing on to stagnant water.

‘You should have this. Maybe your father will believe you now.’

This pleased Segun very much. She hugged Tayo, and the rest of us leant in for a group hug.

CHAPTER TWENTY-TWO
BROKEN BREAD

Mama Tea was different this morning. We never got more than, 'Good morning, fine girl' or a smile and a nod, but today she swayed from side to side, singing and talking as she poured tea from her stove kettle into mugs.

'Ssh!' Tayo said to Gemini and me who were not paying attention. 'Listen to Mama Tea's song.'

'Huh?' Gemini didn't understand.

'Listen!' Tayo insisted.

Gemini and I leant in. It took me a while to catch the words with all the racket in the dining hall, but as she poured tea in my own mug, I made out the words.

Rats with tails and rats without
Clean our river or we will shout
Bribery here and corruption there
War on the bakery, we declare!

'C'mon!' Mama Tea added just before she went into the chant again.

'Mama Tea! Where did you hear that song?' Tayo asked.

Mama Tea was only too eager to tell us. 'Ah last night o, in the town ni. All those acada boys and girls like you. They said they are not going to school again unless we sign paper. They have vexed! They were shouting it up and down carrying cardboard. Me I signed well, well! I am tired of no water.'

I could not believe what I was hearing. 'This must be Segun and her friends!' I screamed with glee.

Gemini, Tayo and I were so thrilled by this news that we put down our tea and hugged Mama Tea.

This pleased her so much that she topped up our teas and we had to walk extremely slowly to our tables.

When we got to the room one table, we taught Dongo, Caro and Tope the chant. Tope made a beat with her spoon and before we knew it, the whole dining hall was singing it:

Rats with tails and rats without . . .

The beating of spoons and hands on the tables made it even more exciting and soon the whole hall was dancing. The other kitchen ladies came into the dining hall and looked on in amusement.

Rashidat came to the front and began to show the actions that she had made up in less than a minute. She wagged her hand behind her for a tail and then raised it again. She dipped one hand in the other for 'bribery' and the opposite hands for 'corruption' and then she raised both hands in the air to declare war. Everyone was now on their feet and different people kept coming up to our table to ask questions about what was going on and what the song meant. Even Dongo was deep in conversation explaining all the things that had been going on along the river.

If it weren't for Princey who came into the dining hall a few minutes later, we would not have stopped. The song was so catchy, it made me want to stand in front of the bakery and shout at the top of my voice.

'Girls, girls, settle down.' Princey's voice finally made its way into everyone's ears and we stood in front of our tables.

'Mama Tea has informed me that no one is eating the bread from Redbrick Bakery this morning. Is this true?'

I looked round. Not a single loaf of bread had been touched and everyone was nodding. My tummy made a long loud growl and everybody began to giggle.

Tayo brought out the photos from her school bag. 'Let's show Princey these now,' she said to us.

'Yes!' shouted Tope, surprising us all.

I guess our protests had warmed everyone's belly.

Tope, Gemini and I followed Tayo towards Princey. I could feel everyone's eyes on us wondering what we were up to next.

'Ma, we have something to show you,' Tayo said and she handed Princey the pictures.

Princey looked at each one intently. When she got to the one with the rat on the fridge, she gasped.

'Ma, the bakery is using the river as a rubbish

dump,' Tayo explained. 'These are the pictures we took and . . .' Tayo's voice faded away as she realized she would have to explain where she got the photos from.

'How have the authorities let this happen and how can Mr Hassan stand to live like this?' Princey was muttering to herself.

'But Ma! The rubbish heap is not on his side of the river. It's right here at the back of the borehole. Look!' I was all fired up and my words were all jumbled together. I showed her the borehole in the distance in one of the photos.

Princey pulled the photo close to her face and took off her glasses. 'Ah oti o!' She could not believe her eyes.

Mama Tea came and stood beside Princey. 'Yes Ma, we saw a picture like this in the town yesterday. The students were showing it to everybody. Ah Ma, look at that rat. Ehn, rats with tails!' A flash of realization flooded Mama Tea's face.

'I will make sure all this is sorted out,' said Princey firmly. 'I will talk to Mr Eruku and—'

We did not let her finish that sentence.

'Mr Eruku has been given a fat brown envelope

by Mr Hassan! And he said he would look the other way!' Gemini cried.

Princey looked at each one of us and then round the whole school.

'You found out all this on your own?'

We nodded.

'And you mean to keep to your protest about the bread?'

This time, the dining room resounded with a loud 'Yes!'

'Since you are boycotting the bread, fruits and snacks from town will be sent to your classrooms. Mama Tea, perhaps we can have an early lunch?'

Mama Tea nodded vigorously. 'Yes Ma.'

We broke into applause and soon the whole dining room was clapping and cheering.

'You may go to your classes, girls,' Princey said quietly. Her eyes were full of pride.

We filed out, and I breathed a big sigh of relief. Thanks to Segun and her friends, the protest about the Redbrick Bakery had spread to the River School. And best of all, now Princey was on our side.

CHAPTER TWENTY-THREE
EXAMS GALORE!

We only had two weeks left before exams and so we had to put all excitement aside and try to concentrate on our studies. Caro and Tayo really tried to help me with last-minute reading all through the night and many tutorials to get me through maths. Our exams had been scheduled to coincide with the end of the seniors' exams. When we finished ours, we went over to the Great Hall to wait for them to come out.

We had already made paper graduation hats and carried rice in little containers that Mama Tea had given us. Once we got to the area of the hall where the seniors were taking exams, we had to be very quiet. Many teachers were outside the hall making sure.

'I can't wait to be in my final year at River School,' Bukky said.

'Me, I can wait.' I flashed my teeth at her and made a face.

'I can't wait to be in Form Three which is statistically—' Tayo was about to go off on one of her long explanations but the bell stopped her. That marked the end of the seniors' exams and we moved like a swarm of bees to the entrance of the Great Hall.

We could hear movement from inside and I was so excited that I was in front. I wanted to see Ngozi who had just completed her mocks and Senior Funmi and Moradeke who had completed their final papers in secondary school. They could be anything they wanted to be from fire chiefs to canoe riders and I wanted to be there to cheer them on.

Someone raised a chant.

No more tests, you are the best!
Come on and beat your chest!

We repeated it until the first senior emerged from the hall and then another. Once there was a steady stream of them trooping out, we began to throw rice at them, still chanting and clapping. We waited until Nile House seniors in their full green-and-white school uniforms surrounded their Nile House supporters in our orange check dresses. Then we threw our decorated paper graduation hats in the air singing:

Winner ooo Winner!
Winner ooo Winner!
Seniors you don win o, Winner!
Pátápátá, you go win for ever, Winner!

We walked and talked with them back to the dorms.

'All I'm going to do is eat and sleep for the rest of term.' Senior Funmi beat her chest as she spoke.

'I am going to play so hard you will think they are paying me to do it,' Ngozi added.

'Nobody should wake me up for anything. I am sleeping until my parents come and drag me from my bed. In fact, I am already sleeping right now!' We roared with laughter as Senior Moradeke started making dramatic snoring sounds.

My cheeks were hurting from smiling when we got to the path that led to the dorms. Parked right by Nile House was the fire truck. Several of us rushed towards the chief who was sitting in the vehicle reading a paper. She jumped out of the truck when she saw us.

'Well done on completing your exams,' she said, lifting her hands into the air. I jumped up to slap my palms against hers. The seniors were scattered all around enjoying their freedom and there was still a buzz in the air. Caro was the first to spot the Atlantic Four walking towards the seniors.

'Look!' she cried so loud that it made all of us turn.

'They've got Riro!' It was my turn to shriek.

As soon as they saw us, Yinka began to call out to the seniors. She let her three followers carry the grey bowl with Riro inside. Several girls had crowded round Riro cooing and stroking her.

'Senior Moradeke, did you know that your

room one girls have been keeping a pet under their beds?' Yinka said, looking around to see the shock on everyone's face.

'Is that so?' Senior Moradeke said in a very exaggerated tone.

'It is so!' said Follower One and Two together.

Yinka had picked the wrong time to report us to the seniors. They were in no mood to take anything seriously.

Ola had joined in stroking the turtle and Yinka elbowed her back to her senses.

'Yes, I'm tired of all the stealing that has gone on in Nile House,' Ola blurted out clumsily.

Senior Moradeke rolled her eyes and Nile House girls began to murmur their outrage.

Finally, the chief, who had not taken her eyes off Riro for a second, looked up. 'Who took this creature out of the river?' she asked, looking around at all of us.

Nobody said it was them.

'I *wish* it was me,' Gemini said.

And that paved the way for Caro and Dongo to own up. As soon as they raised their hands, Yinka jumped in.

‘I knew you would be involved! There was no stealing before you arrived,’ she said to Dongo, looking her up and down.

‘I don’t agree that they stole anything. I wanted to congratulate them,’ the chief replied.

‘What?’ Yinka snarled incredulously.

‘Well, yes! You managed to save at least one creature from that mess going on in the river.’ The chief smiled and continued. ‘In fact, you should keep the turtle until they declare the river safe and ready for the canoe race. Have you given it a name?’

‘Riro!’ all six of us from room one cried.

Once everyone knew its name, they all crowded round the laundry bowl and called out to the turtle.

‘I declare Riro the official Nile House mascot for the term,’ Senior Moradeke announced. This received thunderous applause.

Yinka threw up her hands in frustration. ‘I give up!’ she said and turned back towards Zambezi with her three friends right behind her.

The chief lifted the bowl towards us and Dongo and Caro reached out to collect it.

'Let one of your friends take it,' she said to Dongo. 'I want to talk to you about rowing.'

There was a kind of awed hush as everyone began to look at Dongo with respect.

'Who, me?' Dongo said.

'Yes. I need someone to practise with while Mr Lawanson is on duty here. You are very good with a canoe.'

At first, Dongo looked very shy and unsure.

Senior Moradeke spoke up, a little sparkle in her eyes. 'Hey Dongo, are you *good* at canoe or not?'

Dongo stared back at the senior and then at me and Caro. We nodded back. It seemed that was all she needed.

'I am very good with canoes,' she said with a little more confidence.

'Then *own it*!' Senior Moradeke stamped her foot on the ground for emphasis.

'Please Chief, wait here!' Dongo said, running up the stairs and into the dorm. The Dongo that returned moments later was remarkably different. She held out her rugged notebook in the air.

'We can shave our wooden oars this way so that . . .' Dongo opened up her notebook in front of the chief to reveal page after page of drawings of various canoes. They were so detailed, you would have thought an experienced engineer had drawn them. They were labelled extensively with a thick pencil and she spoke so eloquently about what she would do to get the best from a canoe.

'Did you draw all this yourself, Dongo?' Chief Ogunbanjo started to flip through every page.

'Yes Chief,' Dongo said proudly.

'This is impressive, Dongo. I think we need you on the rowing team for sure. With Mr Hassan rowing for North Side, we're going to need all the help we can get. Come with me, let's go rowing. The rest of you can join us at the river on foot.' Chief Ogunbanjo put on her driving gloves and led Dongo towards the fire truck.

I couldn't believe it. Dongo was the first of us to get a ride in the red shiny truck. A small bout of jealousy came over me but only for a little while, because I realized that a victory for one River School girl was a victory for all.

CHAPTER TWENTY-FOUR
FIRE ON THE MOUNTAIN

I must have been the last to fall asleep. It had been a lovely evening. I wanted to sit back and peel the activities of the day like a tangerine. I'm not sure how long I'd been sleeping for when a siren rang through the whole school. I jumped out of my bed startled. Everyone rushed to Gemini's top bunk to look out of the window. There was a red light swirling over Princey's cottage and several lights started to go on across the school. We grabbed our wrappers and housecoats and went outside. Seniors and juniors from every house littered the pathways between houses.

'There must be a fire nearby,' someone said.

'How do you know? We have never heard that alarm ever since we have been in this school,' another person insisted.

Someone put on a torch and led the way towards the dining hall.

I kept close to my room-mates; they made me feel safe.

As we turned the corner, that was when we saw it. A blaze in the distance like nothing I had ever seen. A bright orange inferno blasting through the skies.

'Fire!' Someone felt the need to spell it out.

'It's Redbrick Bakery!' I shouted, suddenly realizing that was the only thing in that direction.

If there was pandemonium because of the fire, realizing it was the bakery made everyone go absolutely crazy.

A fire truck started to approach our rowdy group and we crowded round it hungry for information.

Princey emerged from the truck with Chief Ogunbanjo. She was dressed in a dark housecoat and a bright coloured hairnet, and the chief was fully dressed in a thick luminous yellow fire jacket and matching trousers.

'Good evening, girls.' The chief's assured tone gave me immediate comfort. 'As you can tell, there is a fire. I was delivering water to the principal when I saw it. I have alerted the fire department and the fire officers are on their way to the bakery. I think you are all OK so I will join them there now . . .'

'Don't worry, everything will be all right,' Princey told us.

Several of our housemistresses started to arrive in their cars. Mrs Aliu and Mrs Kolawole came out of the same car and hurried towards us. We gathered around them and peppered them with questions.

There was a buzz from the radio attached to the chief's hip and she raised one finger to quieten us. She began to respond to someone on the radio.

'Fire Chief 101. Do you read me? Yes, I hear you loud and clear. On this side of the river? Are you sure? An old bridge. OK, no access! I will see what I can do from this end until you get here. Over and out.'

The chief turned to face the principal. 'Apparently, there is an old bridge that has caught fire on this side of the river and it cannot be accessed from the bakery. Something about many trucks parked on the bridge.'

'We have access to the bridge from behind the borehole,' I said to the chief. 'The old bridge leads from there to the bakery.'

'So there is access to water there too?'

'Yes Chief,' I said.

'And are you sure there is access to the bridge?'

Every room one member leapt forward and shouted a resounding 'Yes Chief!'

'We have seen it with our own two eyes!' Tayo said passionately.

Chief Ogunbanjo looked at the principal.

'That is where all the rubbish has been dumped by the bakery,' Princey said sadly.

'Ma, I will have to go there at once!'

'You are not going without me!' Princey said most assuredly.

'Jummy, get into the front with Mrs Ayodele and those of you that have seen this bridge, get into the back of the truck,' the fire chief ordered.

I climbed into the truck and was soon sandwiched between Princey and the chief. Gemini,

Tayo, Dongo, Caro and Tope jumped into the back.

Nobody said a word as the truck raced to the borehole gates behind the dining hall. I was both giddy with excitement and petrified by what we might find on the bridge. I looked at the dashboard of the fire truck. There were so many buttons and small screens. The chief handled the truck with such competence that I felt assured that whatever happened tonight, we were going to be all right.

We approached the gates that led to the borehole but the chief did not get down to open them.

'Hold on tight, girls!' she said as she burst through the metal gates and rode up the path that we had gone through so many times this term.

'This is the borehole and up there through those bushes is the bridge!' I shouted above the noise of the truck's engine.

'The river is there too!' Tayo warned.

The chief rode the truck through the bushes and then we were faced with a blaze so large it lit up the whole night sky.

We gasped in horror at the sight.

The chief put on the brightest of her truck

lights and it showed the pathway to the bridge.

'The fire is spreading from the bridge on to the rubbish in the river.' I pointed frantically.

'It's actually the other way round,' the chief said. 'It looks as if the fire started from the rubbish, and we have to make sure it doesn't catch on to the bushes because after that it will spread into the school.'

She peered into the distance. 'Oh my goodness! Who's that?'

A figure was lying close to the bridge – was someone hurt?

She got on her radio immediately. 'Fire Chief 101 . . . do you read me? Please send an ambulance. We have an injured person at the borehole behind the River School. Engage North Side Fire Department immediately. The bakery is not at risk, but the River School is. Over and out!'

The chief jumped out of the truck and ran ahead. We saw her pull the figure away from the bridge and the bushes. The figure seemed to be moving a little, but I couldn't tell any more.

Princey got out too. 'Girls, stay in the truck!' she said firmly.

'Jummy, can you see who it is? Who is injured?' Gemini asked from the back and that was when I saw the green kaftan.

My heart sank. I did not say a word. I could not tell Tope that her dad was the injured man. At least, not yet.

The chief returned to us, leaving Princey with Mr Lawanson. She told us to get out and head to the borehole. I think she just wanted to keep us from knowing who the injured man was. I prayed with all my might that he would be OK.

She began to unroll the hose and we did what we were told.

'I've only half a tank of water in the truck. We need to get the water direct from the borehole.' The chief thought for a while. 'I suspect because of the low water levels, that may be a problem. Take me there and let us see.'

Dongo led the way to the borehole. The chief pulled open the concrete lid with ease and flashed her heavy-duty torch down into the borehole.

'It's like I thought. The level of water in the borehole is not high enough . . .'

'Look!' Gemini pointed.

A sea of torchlights was swimming quickly along the path towards us.

It looked like every single girl in the River School had come to help. Seniors and juniors alike. As they got closer we could see they all carried an empty bucket in their hands. Gone were the housecoats and wrappers. Each girl was dressed as we would on labour day when we cut the grass around the school in long trousers and tops.

'This is excellent!' the chief cried. 'I have never seen this kind of courage in all my years as a fire chief.'

She looked at all six of us. 'Mobilize them as I try to hose down the fire – we need to refill the tank of the truck.'

'Yes Chief!' we cried in unison.

The chief drove the truck as near as she could to the bridge and let up the ladder of the fire truck.

Dongo went down the borehole with Caro at first but throughout the night, different girls took turns in filling the buckets. I carried buckets to the truck's tank along with many other girls, and

Tayo and Gemini were responsible for pouring the water into the top of the tank of the fire truck.

It felt like for ever before another set of fire trucks arrived at the scene and we could stop fetching water. We stood back and let the fire department take over. The ambulance followed swiftly behind and that was when we saw Princey again. She and Mrs Aliu took Tope aside and spoke to her. Mrs Aliu wrapped her in a blanket as all the room one girls looked on.

'Her dad is the injured man.' I finally could let the words out.

We all ran towards Tope to comfort her.

'He is going to be all right. Just some minor injuries and smoke inhalation,' Mrs Aliu reassured us. 'The ambulance will take him to hospital.'

Tope rested her head on Gemini's shoulder as we watched the fire go down finally.

The chief came and stood before us. 'River School girls, it is my pleasure to announce the fire is out and there have been no fatalities!'

The roar and cheers that reverberated across the night was electric. We hugged each other and clapped for what seemed to be a lifetime. We didn't want to stop. The ambulance purred into life and the chief called Tope to see her dad. 'Would you like to ride with him?'

'Yes Chief.' Tope nodded.

We followed the ambulance for a while until we heard Princey's voice. Mrs Kolawole had handed her a loudspeaker.

'Girls, I have never been prouder of you than I am tonight. You are a remarkable bunch of young women who have shown courage and unity when others would have chosen fear. Have a good night's rest. It is breakfast in bed for you all later in the morning and no schoolwork at all!'

We cheered with delight one more time and I knew instantaneously what to do with my big lungs. We all belted out the chorus of the school song as we made our way back to our dorms.

Together, we truly shine
For victory is yours and mine
Shine River School, River School shine!

CHAPTER TWENTY-FIVE
CORN, THIS WAY!

Ever since the fire, there had been a real sense of camaraderie in the whole school. It didn't seem to bother anyone which house they were in. Nile House room one was always heaving with girls from different houses who wanted to know when Tope would be back. She had gone home to stay with her family. All we knew was that her dad was not in a critical state any more but still recovering in hospital. And everyone wanted to come into our room to stroke Riro, including the seniors.

Today was the day we would harvest our corn and present it to Princey and the teachers who would decide which house had grown the best corn. Several houses were already out harvesting and some had even started preparing their presentation stalls in the gardens in front of their houses. Someone said Tope might arrive today and we thought it was only right to wait for her.

'Maybe we should just start and then she can join us when she gets here?' Tayo said, looking through the window.

'Yes, we could start removing the corn at least.' Caro joined Tayo at the window looking very worried.

'OK let's do it!' Gemini jumped off her bed.

We all agreed and followed Gemini out on to the lawn. She had just braced herself to call the others out on to the lawn when someone spoke behind us.

'What on earth are you doing?' It was Tope standing there with her hands on her hips.

We all hugged her and fussed over her. Bukky came out into the corridor and when she saw her, screamed '*Tope Lawanson!*' so loudly and with so much glee that everybody heard and rushed out.

'How is Mr Lawanson?' Caro asked and everybody started to ask the same thing instead of waiting for an answer.

'My dad is on the mend,' Tope answered, smiling broadly.

Before we could smother her with more hugs, she added, 'So let's get harvesting! Get all your tools and meet at the back. Appropriate clothes unless you want scorpions to bite you.'

'She's *back*!' somebody shouted, and we all dispersed cheerfully.

Tope led all Nile House girls to the corn plants at the back of our dorm. Every single one of us had been responsible for watering and weeding over the last few weeks. Tope, Gemini, Tayo and I showed the others what we had learnt from the bakery farm and soon our large basket was full of corn.

'Wooooo! Look at that!' Gemini had come over to help us in the Form One section. She was pointing to Caro's part of the ridge. There were the last two of Caro's corn plants and they were the largest corn cobs we had seen on our entire set of ridges.

'These are going to be the ones we showcase,' Tope said, taking the corn from Caro and showing them to everyone.

'My mother would be so proud,' Caro said, beaming with pride.

Two Form Three girls carried the large basket to the front of Nile House and we began to decorate our garden with the orange heliconias with corn plants and cobs. Tope used string to create a line with corn hanging from it. We also housed the corn in orange buckets but for Caro's big corn cobs, we brought out my locker and covered it with my orange check bedspread. Then we placed the cobs with their silks still intact on the locker in an attractive pile.

As if that weren't already grand enough, Tope went in and returned with two pieces of black cloth which she used as a drape to keep our display a surprise.

'You don't want to give it all away yet!' she said to us. 'Now go around and see what the rest look like.' She laughed and stuck her tongue out at us. I was so glad to have her back.

We first went to Congo House who had some pretty big corn but definitely not as big as Caro's. Then we went through to Limpopo and Senegal who had pretty much the same as Congo House.

'We are going to smash this out of the park!' Gemini whispered to me.

When we got to the Zambezi stall, there was a larger crowd of girls surrounding their garden of hibiscus. They had designed the whole garden with their red check bedspreads and used them to lay the corn in mounds. Then in the middle of the garden was someone's locker just like ours with several corn cobs on top. The corn they displayed was the largest set of corn you ever saw. They were even larger than the ones we had seen at Redbrick Bakery.

My mouth dropped. I looked around for Gemini. I could see her walking into Zambezi House with intent. I chased after her and called her name. She didn't answer.

I ran towards Tope who was just arriving at the Zambezi stall with other Nile House girls.

'Look at their stand – it's an exact replica of ours,' I said to her.

Her mouth dropped just like mine had done earlier.

'Gemini has gone into Zambezi House. I don't

need to explain to you what may take place,' I said, trying to convey the seriousness of the situation without spelling it out.

Tope immediately understood and headed up the Zambezi House stairs. When we both got inside, there were raised voices coming from one of the rooms.

We followed the noise and had to push past some girls who were standing outside listening.

We found Gemini in the centre of three Zambezi girls and one Nile House girl, Ola. The Atlantic Four looked ready for war but Gemini was holding her own.

'You *copied* our exact presentation. Can't you be a little bit original?' Gemini said.

'Who's to say you didn't copy us?' Yinka shot back.

'That's right!' Ola said and was about to continue but Tope cut her short.

'Hold on a minute, Ola! What is all this business of following Zambezi girls around? Sure, you can have friends in other houses but not to the detriment of your own house.'

'Wherever the Atlantic Four go, I go.' Ola stuck

her thumb into her chest.

'Did you know that the Pacific Ocean is larger than the Atlantic Ocean?' We hadn't seen Tayo come into the room.

'Oh Tayo!' Every person in the room protested but it was the perfect thing to defuse the situation.

'Look, you can copy us all you want and Ola, you can ditch your house all you want but at the end of the day . . .'

Just then, Caro and Dongo ran into the room.

'Princey is here! She is starting with us!' Caro said urgently.

Yinka gave a long drawn-out hiss. 'Please leave our room immediately!'

'With pleasure,' Gemini said before we all left.

We rushed back to Nile House just in time to meet Princey, all the housemistresses, Mr Okocha and Mr Ademola the agricultural science teacher.

'Good afternoon, Ma!' we all said.

'Welcome to the Nile House corn presentation,' Tope said, lifting the black cloth to reveal our corn. After we had left to look at the other houses, Tope must have pulled back the ears of the corn halfway and then tied large orange bows on them.

Everyone started oohing and aahing at our corn.

'Some impressive planting going on here,' Princey said, picking up one of the corn cobs and turning to Mrs Aliu.

'Very impressive indeed,' Mr Ademola said, also examining one of the corn cobs.

'Yes, the girls have worked really hard. I am very proud of them.' Mrs Aliu nodded smugly.

Some of the seniors started to pat Tope on the shoulders and she smiled back at them proudly.

'Shall we see the others?' Princey said to the teachers.

Many of us followed the adults round the houses to hear their comments and it was a very enjoyable afternoon with lots of laughter.

Finally, we headed to Zambezi House.

'They will have to have corn as big as elephants to outshine Nile House,' a girl from Congo said to me.

We got to the Zambezi House display before the adults and met the Atlantic Four guarding their corn display with interlocked arms.

'I can still see.' Gemini made a face at them.

The adults arrived and only then did the four

girls make way for the judges.

If there was a gasp at the sight of our own corn, there was an even louder whoop at the sight of the Zambezi House corn. They looked so large and full of juicy corn kernels. They were the most perfect corn I had ever seen.

Princey felt the same way and she reached out to touch one of them just like she had at all the other presentations.

Yinka pushed forward and smiled sweetly. 'Ah Ma, you don't want to dirty your hands.' But Princey was determined to touch the perfect cobs.

As soon as she had her hand on it, she frowned and turned it over. The back was not as perfect as the front. In fact, there were barely any kernels at the back and the few that were there were brown and tiny.

Mr Ademola looked surprised. 'What happened? Did you not water the plants?'

Ola, in a complete panic and totally forgetting she wasn't in Zambezi, pushed forward. 'We did sir, we even put NPK fertilizer and—'

Yinka dug her elbow into Ola and so she stopped speaking.

'Wait, you did *what*?!' The agricultural science teacher sounded shocked. 'I never gave you permission to do that. I already put enough NPK in the soil before you planted the seeds. No wonder, this is a result of too much fertilizer.' He lifted the corn cob into the air for everyone to see.

'Oh dear! Well, we had better get on with judging and announcing the winner,' Princey said, walking away with the teachers.

Everyone fell silent as the realization of what the four girls had done hit the other Zambezi House girls. They were fuming. Chichi looked as if she wanted to punch someone.

Three of the Atlantic Four were crestfallen. They bowed their heads as the judges left. I felt very sorry for them but Yinka was livid.

'We should have never allowed you in our group, Ola. You are so stupid! Couldn't you keep your mouth shut?' She spoke so rudely, I wanted to shake the girl to come back to her senses.

Yinka continued to rain insults on the girl as we all dispersed.

'And I should tell everyone that you're a thief too!'

I stopped dead in my tracks and turned. Nile House girls turned too. Everyone was now looking at the Atlantic Four.

'Yes, she stole the gold necklace from Senior Funmi and tried to frame anyone in room one because she's jealous of you all.'

'Aah!' Dongo cried out.

Ola finally couldn't take it any more. She beat her chest with her hand. 'I never did any such thing. It was you. *You* stole the gold chain, *you* stole the turtle and *you* stole NPK fertilizer from the agric lab!'

We all gasped and stared at Yinka. Senior Moradeke and the Zambezi House captain drew closer and were about to intervene.

'And Ola stole Jummy's ten naira too,' Yinka spat out venomously. Everyone turned to look at me.

The truth of the matter suddenly became very clear to me.

'I never told anyone how much was stolen from me,' I said.

That was the sentence that sealed Yinka's fate. The disdain on everyone's face said it all.

Yinka just stood there and couldn't say anything.

'Come with me, Yinka, you have some explaining to do.' The Zambezi House captain, a very severe-looking senior, took her by the hand and led her towards Mrs Kolawole, their housemistress.

Senior Moradeke moved towards Ola and put her arm around her. 'Why don't you stick with your own house from now on?' Her gentleness surprised me.

'I just wanted to be part of something special,' Ola said, still sniffling and tearful.

'Look around you, my dear,' Senior Moradeke said. 'You *are* part of something special.'

Princey stood on the Nile House stairs to address us, the seniors quietening us down.

'River School girls, this term you have outdone yourselves and shone like stars. I don't even know how you managed to grow corn under such difficult circumstances. From the water crisis, to boycotting delicious food and then coming together to put out the fire. You are all amazing. I want to assure you that investigations are underway. The police are looking into corruption at the Water Authorities and also into what started the fire at the back of our school. They have assured me that the river will be ready for the canoe race and those responsible for its pollution will be brought to justice.'

Once I heard the canoe race was still going ahead, I raised my hand without hesitation.

'Yes, Jummy.' Princey calling me Jummy gave me all the confidence I needed.

'But who will row the canoe with the chief now?' A quiet hum passed across the front of Nile House.

'I was going to save that for the next assembly but I might as well let you know that the chief herself has recommended that Dongo Karkananshi will be the second person to row the South Side canoe.'

Usually, we would cheer loudly but there was something remarkable about this evening and gentle applause seemed much more appropriate. Everyone looked at Dongo who was just a few rows behind me in the crowd. She smiled a toothless smile at us.

‘Once again, River School girls, you should be very proud of all you have accomplished this term. Give yourselves another round of applause – you deserve it!’

I looked around as we applauded ourselves. The judges joined Princey on the stairs. They announced Nile House as the winners of the corn-planting competition and the whole crowd rejoiced as if everyone was a winner.

Senior Moradeke was right. We were all part of something truly special.

CHAPTER TWENTY-SIX
CANOE RACE

The day we had been waiting for all term had finally arrived. It was time for the canoe race. I looked out of the window. The weather did not disappoint. The sun stood majestically in the sky and as if that weren't already good enough, somebody screamed: 'There's water running from the taps!'

That was all we needed. Everyone jumped from their beds to see the sight that had eluded us almost all term.

There was of course a long queue for the showers but when it was finally my turn, it was worth the wait. I let the water soak through my afro and I just stood there and enjoyed every minute.

There was a loud bang on my shower cubicle door.

'Jummy, come and see what the chief sent for Dongo. She's leaving in a few minutes. Quick!'

It was Caro and her excitement that brought me back to my senses.

I wrapped my towel around me and walked quickly back to our room. There were several girls outside trying to peek inside.

'Nile House, room one girl coming through,' I called out as I wriggled through them.

When I got into the room, Dongo was already dressed. My heart skipped a few beats at the sight of her. She was dressed in green trousers with white stripes on either side. It made her legs look even longer than they already were. A white pair of plimsolls sat neatly on her feet and she wore a green polo top. A green cap completed the ensemble.

Then, she turned round so I could see the words written on the back of her top: 'South Side for the Win'.

'Doesn't she look incredible?' Caro asked,

stating the obvious.

'Yes, she does! Dongo, you look *perfect*,' I added, remembering to grab Owolabi's camera.

'She looks like those athletes at the Olympics when they come up for their trophy.' Gemini was getting dressed too. All of us were going to be dressed in house skorts and polo tops.

'I'll take that as a sign of victory!' Dongo said and she gave Gemini a high five.

Chief Ogunbanjo came for Dongo in a regular car and we all went out and cheered them off with the chief honking her horn all the way past the dining hall.

As we left, Tope and a few other Form Three girls handed out baskets of corn for us to carry to the river. Tope had put her whole self into every activity there was. I think she was trying not to think of her father. He was getting better but Princey had said it was a long, slow road to recovery. Tope told us that the police had come to see him but he was still unable to talk to them.

I carried a basket with Caro.

'I thought it would be heavier than this,' I said as soon as I lifted it up.

'It's heavy enough,' Bukky said, walking behind me with Flanky.

Barky darted from Princey's garden and followed us. Michelle carried her almost all the way to the river, much to the annoyance of Tayo who ended up bearing the weight of their basket of corn alone.

The whole school was making their way to the river. We hadn't seen it since the Water Authorities had inspected it and cleared it for the race.

Only Dongo and a few others had been allowed to practise rowing there with the chief. We had played all our end-of-year games in the big open space behind the assembly ground.

We moved tentatively towards the top of the hills where everyone had left their baskets of corn for Mama Tea to pick up with the kitchen van. I closed my eyes and breathed in deeply, waiting for the river to greet us in whatever manner it chose. The first thing that was different was the glorious smell of nothing.

I opened my eyes to the wonder that always mesmerized us as we mounted the bridge on the first day of term. The wonder that had, like our shower water, eluded us all term.

Shine-Shine River glistened under the sun and splashes of sunlight reflected on its surface just like old times. I lifted Owolabi's camera up – click!

'Look!' Tayo shouted. '*Leke Leke!*'

Every single one of us ran down the hills towards our beloved river, to meet the beautiful white egrets that the myth said could deposit white streaks on your fingernails if you sang a song to them.

The playground had been transformed too. There were several barbecue stations set up to roast corn and each house had a large bright coloured marquee erected. We walked straight to the bright orange one on the far right of the playground. There were many Nile House girls sitting on cushions that had been provided.

'Let's go and see Dongo,' Caro begged me. I didn't need to be convinced. I wanted to see her and the chief before the race started as well.

We walked down to the riverfront. There were two other men with Chief Ogunbanjo and Dongo.

The chief was dressed exactly like Dongo. Her muscles protruded from the green polo top sleeves. She looked awesome.

'Hello girls. Meet the officers of the South Side Fire Department,' the chief said.

'Good morning sir, good morning sir,' we greeted the two men.

They nodded and continued to attend to the canoe and oars. The canoe was painted green and white too, just like their clothes. Dongo was sitting in another canoe by the shore.

'Good luck, Dongo,' we both said to her as we approached.

'Thank you, my friends. You know whatever happens, I will remember this day for ever. The day I got to do what my father spent his whole life doing.'

'We will take lots of pictures. Don't worry!' I pointed to the camera around my neck.

'Take a picture now,' Caro nudged.

'Ah yes, why not.'

We posed together and I tried to take it facing the other way so that I could get into the picture but with a Polaroid camera it was very difficult.

'Let me take a picture of all of you. Chief, get in the picture.' To my surprise, it was Ola extending her arm towards me. Her hair was neatly plaited into six simple cornrows and she wore an orange headband.

Caro and I smiled at each other.

'That's very kind, Ola. Thank you,' I said cheerfully.

Dongo stayed sitting in the canoe while the chief stood in between Caro and me. She put her arm around us. We felt so proud already and the race had not even started.

Click! Ola handed me the photo she had taken along with the camera. I was going to miss it when Owolabi came for it.

'We better let you get on,' I said, squeezing Dongo's shoulder.

Several more girls and teachers had now arrived at the playground and it was bursting. People sat on the hillside, under the marquees and all around the top of the hills. The other side of the river was filling up too with a mixed crowd of North and South Side supporters.

Music started to play from the Shine-Shine bridge where the competition would begin. Dongo got out of the practice canoe and she and the chief got into the green-and-white canoe.

There was some excitement behind us and I turned to see a black car followed by two coaches approaching from the road at the top of the hill. The coaches were full to the brim with Kingswill college boys who were already getting out of their seats before the vehicles had come to a stop just shy of the river. Many of us started walking towards them once we saw Mrs Ayodele and some other teachers doing so.

Mr Davies, the Kingswill College principal, came out of the black car with two other adults. He shook hands with Princey.

Mr Davies looked at our rowers and smiled. 'South Side for the win!'

A few of us cheered and grinned at each other.

'You know we are always on the same side.' Princey smiled back. 'Come with me sir, we are sitting under the white canopy.' She turned to us. 'Please make the boys feel welcome.'

The boys were already mingling.

'Hey, you look way too comfortable with that thing around your neck.' Owolabi was in front of me in an instant. He gently took the camera off my neck and I blushed a little.

'Ahem!' Gemini coughed.

I looked at her as if I had been caught with my hands in another person's packet of plantain chips.

One of the firemen blew a whistle which brought everyone's attention to the fact that the rowers were starting their journey to the bridge.

Boys and girls alike came towards the river-bank to see them off. We cheered as the two firemen pushed the canoe into the river, Dongo and the chief already rowing. We followed them on foot until there was no shoreline left.

Gemini nudged me. 'Is that Mr Eruku getting into the canoe with Mr Hassan?'

I looked at the shiny bald head in the distance and shrugged.

'Whatever happens, we are on the better team!'

CHAPTER TWENTY-SEVEN
CROSSING THE BRIDGE

There were hundreds and hundreds of people on the bridge waving flags and posters, supporting each side. Several minutes passed before the music stopped and a familiar voice started speaking on a public address system. It was Mr Okocha.

'Good morning, North Side!' he cried, and there was a huge roar of support from the other side of the river and the bridge. I imagined Mr Hassan and his bribed bandits snarling like wolves.

'Good morning, South Side.' The combination of all of the River School and over a hundred Kingswill boys filled the air with a deafening sound fit for an Olympic arena.

Caro covered her ears and I roared louder than I ever had before.

'Welcome to the Ogun State Canoe Race. Are the rowers ready?'

Everyone cheered again.

'On your marks . . . get set . . . *go*!'

The two canoes began their journey up the river. They would row all the way round to the end and row right back to the bridge.

'They will put a ribbon across the river so that there will be no doubts about the winner,' Tayo informed us.

When the canoes went past us again, we ran all the way to the end of the shoreline on the other side of the playground and cheered South Side on. Our green-and-white canoe shone in the distance.

We stood there for a while, laughing and chatting, but soon enough we dispersed into different areas of the playground, while we waited for the canoes to come back.

'So is the corn for only River School girls?' Owolabi said, sniffing the smell of delicious roasted corn.

I shrugged. 'Let's find out.'

Owolabi called to his friends, 'There might be some corn on offer!'

We became quite a large group as the three boys joined the room one girls heading towards the barbecue.

Several cobs of corn were roasting, beside them a purple fruit. They looked like tiny purple sausages.

'Oooooh, ube! This is my favourite thing to eat with roasted corn.' Caro curtseyed to the lady and this warmed the woman's heart to no end.

'My child, take for your friends.' She picked up a square leaf from a basket to her right and put a steaming hot corn cob on it with some ube. She leant over to another basket to her left to reveal several pieces of freshly cut coconut pieces.

'Ah this is heaven!' Caro yelped. 'Thank you, Ma.' She curtseyed again.

The rest of us followed suit, curtseying and bowing to curry the lady's favour, and it worked. We left the canopy with our leaves full of the glorious treat.

Caro showed us how to eat it.

'Make sure you get corn and ube in your mouth at the same time. Kai, it is sweet!' Caro was munching and talking at the same time, looking very unCaro-like.

When I bit into the hot ube, it felt like someone had mashed the richest butter with the smoothest avocado in the world. I bit into some roasted corn at the same time and fell silent. The tanginess of the ube and the sweetness of the roasted corn was heavenly.

'This is really good!' Owolabi said, also munching away happily.

'Your school knows how to put on a good show,' one of Owolabi's friends said.

'The canoes are neck and neck!' shouted Tayo, running towards us. 'They are coming back this way.'

'That was quick!' Owolabi waved his camera in the air and pulled me by the arm. We ran towards the river. The two canoes were just appearing. The trumpets, talking drums and tambourines began making loud music from the bridge again. We started chanting.

'South Side for the win! South Side for the win.'

A black ribbon had been tied on either side of the bridge and we waited in anticipation to see which canoe would tear through it.

As the two canoes got to us, it was not easy to see who was winning. Both canoes seemed to be truly neck and neck. There was no mistaking the daunting figure in the opponent's canoe. It was Mr Hassan and the bald-headed man *was* Mr Eruku.

Suddenly, Dongo stood up tall and then quickly went into a squat. The canoe shook a little but she managed to steady herself. She stood upright again, this time digging both her oars into the water. The two canoes were approaching the ribbon at an equal pace. Then we heard a familiar eerie cry. It was that African fish eagle! It must have flown down from one of the trees. It swooped just above Dongo's head and she ducked low to avoid it – causing her to dig her oars even deeper into the water. That sudden push was all she needed.

The South Side canoe pushed through the black ribbon first.

Mr Hassan got up and flung his hat off angrily.

His bald partner attempted to get up too but their canoe could not handle that and both men toppled over.

There was laughter, there were tears as a deafening roar reverberated all along the waterfront. We didn't know which made us happier, the sight of Mr Hassan bobbing up and down in the river he had nearly ruined, or Dongo and the chief winning the canoe race.

The bellows from the bridge and the opposite side, combined with the noise from the River School was sure to ring through every home in the surrounding area.

Mr Okocha waved his loudspeaker in the air before speaking into it.

'The winner of the Ogun State Canoe Race is . . . the South Side!'

We ran as far as we could along the riverbank, cheering and screaming our heads off. Dongo and the chief would lift the canoe trophy!

Owolabi stood still on a hill capturing it all on his camera. I admired his ability to concentrate enough to capture perfect moments like these.

The noise of a siren filled the air and we turned

to see a rescue boat speeding towards the bridge. We were so excited that we cheered for that too. Mr Hassan and his partner were helped into it.

All the room one girls gathered once again.

'Ladies and gentlemen, boys and girls. I present to you the winning rowers of the Ogun State Canoe Race: Dongo Karkananshi from the River School and Chief Moni Ogunbanjo, South Side Fire Chief!'

Tope, Gemini, Caro, Tayo and I were full of emotion as the chief and Dongo lifted the trophy into the air. I didn't get any warning from my throat; the tears just ran down my face unashamedly.

'I'm so happy, I'm even celebrating that Mr Hassan was rescued,' Caro said.

'That was no rescue boat,' Tayo said emphatically. 'That was the police!'

CHAPTER TWENTY-EIGHT
THE BONGAFISH CHRONICLES

Today was speech and prize-giving day for the seniors and the day before the school holidays. We were still reeling with excitement from winning the canoe race and now we were bidding the seniors farewell.

'Come on, girls! We want the best seats for the press club officials!' Tayo was screeching at us to hurry up.

We marched out quickly with Tayo holding the door for us. She had reserved seats for us press club and she was taking it very seriously.

'I can't reserve seats and now be the last to arrive,' she said as we made our way to the Great Hall.

‘I went to Princey’s office today to speak with my dad. He is sounding much better now,’ Tope told us.

‘Do you know, Tayo, you were right? That was not a rescue boat on the race day. It was the police! They came for Mr Hassan and Mr Eruku!’ Tope was full of information today.

‘I *knew* it! I recognized the police colours,’ Tayo said proudly.

‘What did they arrest them for in the end?’ Caro asked.

‘For destruction of public property and corruption,’ Tope replied. ‘I made sure I asked Daddy everything!’ she added, beating her chest.

‘Mr Hassan was trying to get rid of the rubbish by setting it on fire, but it got out of hand. My dad saw the fire and tried to stop it but the fumes from the rubbish heap ignited more flames. You know the rest.’

‘Oh my goodness!’ Caro exclaimed.

‘I’m glad they didn’t get away with it and justice was served. That doesn’t always happen,’ Dongo said thoughtfully.

‘Justice began with Mr Hassan falling into the

river!' Gemini quipped.

We laughed as that memory filled us with glee. We were silent for the rest of the journey to the Great Hall. Several cars were parked in the visitors area. A senior was walking their parent from the car park into the hall.

'That will be us in a few years. I'm so glad my dad is going to be all right,' Tope said as we climbed the stairs into the hall.

We were one of the last to get there. Everyone was seated and the trophy was on the high table already. To the right, the fire chief sat beside Princey and several other teachers and parents. The press club area was clearly marked on the left. Tayo had made sure of it.

We took our seats while Caro and Dongo left to find other seats.

'Here!' Tayo passed two press club badges to them. 'You are honorary officials now.'

Their eyes shone with so much happiness as they put on their new badges and sat down with us.

Princey walked over to the high table with the six housemistresses. We fell silent. You could hear a pin drop.

'I have never been more proud to send off a set of seniors,' she said. 'These girls were in Form One when I started here as principal and we have come full circle.'

I don't know how Princey did it but every time she spoke, she unlocked something inside of me. I wanted to give my all and do my best.

She began to read out all the seniors' names and they came forward to receive their end-of-school certificates. When she called Senior Moradeke's name we refused to stop clapping, reducing the formidable senior to tears. Princey was in tears too.

Senior Moradeke finally went back to her seat.

'This term has been really hard on you all with water shortages, protests and the fire.' Princey's face became serious all of a sudden and I felt she was looking deep into my soul. My heart began to pound within me.

She looked at each one of us intently for what seemed to be several minutes.

'You girls are incredible,' she finally said. 'The Ministry of Environment has decided to clear the rubbish by the river and use it for a recreational space with trees and park benches for the use of the surrounding towns.'

We all looked at each other proudly.

'Yes, you should be so proud. We have a present for a special set of young women who have gone above and beyond to protect our beloved Shine-Shine River. Can we have all members of the press club up here please?'

We all looked at each other again. We could not believe it. Tayo got up first, then Tope and then all of us stood up. Caro and Dongo were not sure if they were included.

'You've got badges, come on!' I whispered.

We all mounted the stage and joined Princey with all our housemistresses.

'I present you with something that I think you will be very happy with!' Princey smiled as she passed a brown box to Tayo.

Tayo opened it and gasped with pleasure. 'It's a *camera*!' she said, raising it in the air. I was so thrilled, I could hardly contain myself.

The photographer that had been taking all the pictures organized us so we could all fit into one photo.

'Hold on. Chief, come and join us,' Princey said

to the chief who immediately ran up to a cheer from all of us.

The chief picked up the trophy and joined Dongo at the back. I looked at them holding the trophy side by side. This was going to be the perfect picture.

'This is going into the *Bongafish Chronicles*!' Gemini said, and we all burst into laughter as the camera went *click!*

A perfect picture to end a most perfect year indeed.

ACKNOWLEDGEMENTS

To my amazing network of people who make writing in a busy world possible and enjoyable. It is because of their flexibility and belief in me that this book made it to the end. Particularly to my family at home, church and at Chicken House – I give a resounding applause, River School style!